BUILDING
MODEL WARSHIPS
OF THE
IRON AND STEEL ERAS

BUILDING MODEL WARSHIPS OF THE IRON AND STEEL ERAS

Edited by Peter Beisheim

NAVAL INSTITUTE PRESS
Annapolis, Maryland

Frontispiece
A 1/350 scale model of a US Navy *Fletcher* class destroyer of the Second World War,
enhanced with photoetched antennae, and other fine details (see Chapter 6).

Copyright © Chatham Publishing 2002

First published in Great Britain in 2002 by Chatham Publishing,
99 High Street, Rochester, Kent ME1 1LX

Published and distributed in the United States of America, its territories and
possessions, and Canada by Naval Institute Press, 291 Wood Road, Annapolis,
Maryland 21402-5034

Library of Congress Control Number: 2002108322

ISBN 1-59114-094-3

Designed and typeset by Trevor Ridley ATD FRSA
Printed and bound in Great Britain by Bookcraft (Bath) Ltd

Contents

The Contributors

The editor

Peter Beisheim, born in Denmark in 1946, is a lecturer and senior schoolmaster with a life-long interest in naval and military history, his university thesis being on 'The Development of the British Capital Ship 1905-1950', and he has lectured on these subjects at various naval and military museums. He has been scratch-building historical warship models for nearly 25 years, concentrating on Second World War capital ships, and has had articles on ship modelling and naval history published in the magazines *Scale Ship Modeller* and *Ships in Scale*.

The contributors

Philip Baggaley is a retired solicitor and has been a modeller all his life. About 30 years ago he started making models of Second World War warships to the very small scale of 1:1250 and is now on his 10th model. A member of the Society of Model Shipwrights, he has exhibited models at the Model Engineer Exhibition in London, gaining a Gold Medal in the miniature class for the *Alabama* and a Silver Medal for the *Richelieu*.

Eric Dyke is another lifelong modelmaker. Beginning with conversions of Airfix kits in the 1950s and 1960s, he moved on to scratch-building in 1:600 scale, and by the 1970s had built over 100 models. His larger-scale models (1:192) have won many prizes, including a Championship Cup at the Model Engineer Exhibition for his model of HMS *Cavalier*. Despite having retired from competition 10 years ago, he still produces models, many of which are on loan to the Royal Navy. To date he has built 83 models at 1:192 scale

Stephen W. Henninger, a NASA engineer, dedicated his spare time from 1970 to 1982 to building the nuclear carrier *Enterprise* in 1:100 scale. He visited the ship at sea four times from 1975 through 1999, each time as the captain's guest, to add authenticity to the exhibit - even long after its initial display site at the National Air & Space Museum in Washington, D.C, where it has enjoyed extensive popularity with the viewing public. He now builds ship models professionally.

David Jack has been modelling for some 38 years, beginning with Second World War aircraft but a lifelong fascination with wartime MTBs and ASRLs and the development of good-quality modern R/C equipment and motors lead him to working models of these craft at 1:24 scale, which he has been building for 16 years.

Brian King is no newcomer to the model boat scene having built ship models all his life. He has written a large amount for both the North American press as well as here in Britain. He is the author of two books on the subject as well as co-authoring, with Azien Watkin, a book on Photo Etching, a process he uses widely for his own models. He has won many awards nationally at the Model Engineer Exhibition, as well as internationally at Naviga World Championships.

David D Merriman III served in the US Navy for 20 years aboard both conventional and nuclear submarines. He had always built models as a hobby, but later began to develop it into a fully-fledged business, founding D&E Models with his wife Ellie on his retirement. Specialising in R/C submarine kits, his models have featured in a number of films, including the *Hunt for Red October* and *Crimson Tide*.

William Mowll has spent over 30 years making working models of great nineteenth-century ships, namely *Warrior*, *Great Britain* and *Sirius*. He has written two books on this subject, *SS Great Britain: The Model Ship* and *Building a Working Model Warship: HMS Warrior 1860*, as well as numerous articles for ship modelling magazines and journals.

Loren Perry has been building model ships since the early 1950s. His work has been featured in the pages of many hobby magazines over the years, both in the United States and elsewhere, and his model of the US Navy destroyer *Vogelgesang* became the first American model to win a Gold Medal at the prestigious annual Model Engineer Exhibition in England. Mr Perry served as editor of *Scale Ship Modeler* magazine from 1984 to 1992, and runs Gold Medal Models.

Historical Warship Modelling: Naval History in Three Dimensions

by Peter Beisheim

Many years of studying both the collections of maritime museums and model books and magazines have made me realise that strictly historically correct models are still rather atypical. This may surprise many readers who have an interest both in naval history and warship modelling. I have come to appreciate that the majority of older models at least are more like samples of brilliant craftsmanship than the product of historical research. I believe that most modellers have this interest in warship history but, as this book will show, it is time-consuming both to collect and evaluate source material and simultaneously build the model. The difficulties inherent in both building and researching a historical ship often tend to discourage modellers who therefore concentrate most of their efforts into the craftsmanship side of the process.

It is one of the purposes of this book to show that these two approaches to warship modelling are actually compatible. I have always felt that it must be the duty of the warship modeller at least to try to approach historical accuracy as much as possible. In the pursuit of this principle, however, the pleasure of modelling must never be forgotten, as perfectionism carries the unfortunate tendency to kill the joy and satisfaction of the hobby. After a while the dedicated modeller becomes a fanatical

Loren Perry's conversion of the 1:429 scale Revell kit of the battleship USS *Arizona*.

perfectionist unable to complete the model because he cannot meet his own standards. As will appear from these pages historical modelling gives the modeller the opportunity of combining two wonderful hobbies: the study of naval history and the creative pleasure of modelling.

The idea for this book originated from Chatham Publishing's editor Julian Mannering. He approached me a couple of years ago and asked me to write and edit a comprehensive study of historical warship models. We eventually agreed that the book should not cater to the modeller exclusively, but also to the interested layman. In accordance with the historical concept we decided not to concentrate solely on the actual techniques of modelling, but also to feature the development of major warships from the transition from sail to steam and into the nuclear age. It soon became clear that it would be impossible for one individual to cover such a diverse subject with the level of knowledge required, so we asked a group of modellers to write one chapter each and to describe their individual field of interest and techniques. I was given the assignment of editing the combined product and to write, besides my own chapter, the introduction.

In order to be able to produce this book as a coherent work it was imperative to avoid it came becoming a series of more or less uncoordinated articles as one would expect to find in a magazine or a journal. So I had to ask the contributors to agree to describe their approach to certain items consistent with their individual historical period and scale within the context of the book. In more specialised cases, for example miniature modelling or kit conversion, this was not possible, and these chapters cover more or less the modeller's entire method. As the reader will no doubt be able to judge for himself, it was by no means always an easy task to make enthusiastic modellers limit themselves. The popularity of major twentieth century warships, *ie* battleships and aircraft carriers, is inevitably reflected in this book.

Peter Beisheim's model of HMS *Belfast* as in 1943.

However, we saw it as a 'must' that smaller craft also be given fair representation, not least due to their popularity among radio control modellers.

The Contributors

It was agreed to follow the development of the modern warship from the transition from sail to steam, and the beginning of the ironclad period up to the modern nuclear aircraft carrier and submarine. This should give the reader an impression of the diversity of modelling problems and methods in warship modelling. We had already realised that to include all major types of warships from that long period would make the book far too long, so it seemed obvious that HMS *Warrior*, the first iron-built battleship, should be the subject of Chapter 1. Fortunately Will Mowll had already made a name for himself with his both operational and historically accurate model of that ship and kindly agreed to write the first chapter to represent the large scale (1:48) working model, emphasising his hull construction method. The next item on the agenda was logically a late Victorian capital ship to show the incredible development in warship construction in the later nineteenth century. Eric Dyke had already gained international fame for his models and agreed to undertake the (in my eyes) impossible task of both writing Chapter 2 and at the same time building a model of the Victorian battleship HMS *Ocean* in 1:192 waterline. In order not to make the battleship too dominant I decided approach Brian King, whom many readers will know from books and articles and competitions, and ask him to write Chapter 3 to represent the early aircraft carrier HMS *Glorious* in 1:192 as an example of a full hull model and to describe his methods of constructing the flight deck and the aircraft, and his photoetching techniques. To connect the two World Wars and the Dreadnought period HMS *Hood* seemed an obvious choice for Chapter 4 and medium (1:200) scale/static models. In my chapter on the *Hood* I focus on decks and armament of major warships of the inter-war period and the early Second World War.

Since the Second World War seems to be the favourite period for most warship modellers interested in the twentieth-century warship, we were prepared to accept more than one chapter to cover this period. To compensate for this we decided to divide it between several types of warships and vastly different approaches to modelling and scale. Miniature modelling is represented in the book by Philip Baggaley whom many readers will recognise from *Model Shipwright*. Philip's Chapter 5 describes his miniature building and painting techniques in various Second World War battleships and a cruiser in the delicate 1:1250 scale.

Judging from the Internet modelling websites, kit building or kit conversion is immensely popular. I cannot imagine that many warship modellers are unfamiliar with the name of Loren Perry. Not only is Loren a famous modeller, he is also one of the pioneers in the field of photoetching and model photographing. Chapter 6 gives an excellent impression of the potentials of serious plastic kit conversion, and the improvement with photoetched fittings of commercially-produced models. A sometimes neglected topic among those interested in the history of the war at sea are small craft like torpedo boats and subchasers. They have always been very popular among radio-control modellers due to their enormous potential as operational models, not least because of the possibilities of very large scale, such as 1:24. David Jack has been known for his articles in *Marine Modeller* and has done a great job in Chapter 7 describing his hull/engine and detail methods.

In order to find one of the best models of the modern nuclear aircraft carrier one has to go to the Air and Space Museum of the Smithsonian Institution in Washington DC. Stephen Henninger's 1:100 scale USS *Enterprise* (Chapter 8) is on permanent display in their collections, currently located under the wing of Lindberg's *Spirit of St Louis*. Though 1:100 can hardly be called a large scale in itself, the *Enterprise* in that scale is simply huge. Stephen's chapter describes not only the

Philip Baggaley's 1:1250 scale model of IJN *Kitakami*.

David Merriman III's radio-controlled models of US and Soviet submarines.

construction problems of such large and super-detailed models, but also the problems of obtaining reliable plans of warships still in commission.

Submarines have played a major part in naval history, and the modern nuclear submarine dominates, with the nuclear aircraft carrier, modern naval strategy. Since I had already become familiar with 'The Subcommittee' home pages, I knew where to look for a modeller who would be able to cover the modern nuclear submarine in Chapter 9. David Merriman must be known to anyone who is interested in large operational models of submarines, and not least for his model work in such popular movies as *The Hunt for Red October* and *Crimson Tide*.

It would be pretentious to claim that we have covered the majority of classes of warships over more than a century. It is my hope that the reader will see the purpose of this book as we, the writers/modellers, saw it when we started working three years ago: to serve as incitement and inspiration to build historical warship models and, while doing so, gain new friends and contacts among fellow modellers all over the world.

Peter Beisheim
Charlottenlund, Denmark
2002

1
Large-Scale Working Models:
HMS *Warrior* 1860
BY WILLIAM MOWLL

Logic would dictate that those who make models of any kind would be setting out to make an object which was small - pocket-sized even - but modelmakers and miniaturists are much more complex and illogical people than it first appears. Inside the brain of most modelmakers there lurks a dark and dangerous thought that one day they are going to make the big one, the model which will outlast them, and stand as a statement for future generations of just how seriously this so-called hobby was taken when they had the skills and energy to execute the work. And it is very likely that the subject of this *tour de force* will be a warship, because in modelling terms they are the ultimate statement and challenge.

Before setting out on this path of martyrdom, a word or two of caution, words which are particularly aimed at model shipwrights. Building a large model ship will have to fit into your life over a long period of time, say five years, unless you are either a retired person or a professional modelmaker. You will need the agreement of your partner, who must not only put up with you and your absence during this time which you are planning to award yourself, but also face up to the dust and filth and smell which any construction causes as the processes come together. A grudging acceptance of the inevitable is probably the best you can hope for, but at least go for some sort of consultation with your partner, or you will never complete the work, and half-completed masterpieces quickly become dustbin fodder when they fall into enemy hands.

The working environment

Having got the human element sorted out, the maker of large models will also need to be realistic and honest about the space required to carry out the planned work. The workshop space has to fall into a minimum of three categories: the cradle where the model is to be built which must be well-lit; an area for the tools and machinery; and a painted white bench, which is free of clutter, on which the individual pieces may be made. This will more than likely have to serve as the

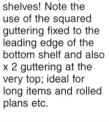

Unbelievably tidy shelves! Note the use of the squared guttering fixed to the leading edge of the bottom shelf and also x 2 guttering at the very top; ideal for long items and rolled plans etc.

A forest of files. Wooden blocks with a handle mean that a full set of files can be brought to the bench. Always make a wooden handle for a needle file. The easy way is to buy a long length of dowel, bore it out and round it off. Very quickly done.

drawing office area, so no tools or machinery must interfere with its flat surface. Add to this the essential need for curtaining off the model from the dust which is being stirred up in the other areas, and the necessity of having access all the way round the object under construction, and you are looking at a large amount of dedicated space. It is a fact of life that models over 5ft in length are going to have to be built off the domestic premises, which means in practical terms a garage or large shed.

There is also the vexed question of shelving. It is not a good idea to have shelving anywhere above or near the working bench, because of vibration, nor should anything be stored above the model up in the rafters. A hot tip with shelving for model boat makers is to employ squared plastic guttering; with its long, thin lengths it is very economical on space and can be fitted to the leading edge of shelving in a most effective way. If at all possible, line the inside of a shed and paint it white. In fact, paint everything white, except a bench top which faces direct sunlight.

In the winter you will have to heat the workshop area to stop your tools and machinery from rusting; it is surprising how a little gentle but constant heat prevents this from happening. More importantly, it encourages you to work consistently through the winter. Be careful that the heating source you use is totally enclosed; oil-filled radiators are the best and safest in amongst all those inflammable paints, etc, although admittedly they are not the most economical form of heating.

Large models, like large trees, grow upwards and outwards, particularly if they are carrying complicated rigging and sail. Make sure that you can get them out of the door without having to alter the masonry. It is a good idea to build a carrying cradle with removable bars immediately the hull is finished as it becomes much more difficult to do this at a later stage. A static model needs to be bolted to the base board early on, for exactly the same reason.

Photography and displaying the model

Begin at the beginning with photography, for two reasons. You will need a record of what you have done, and how you did it, to go with the log notes of your progress. The photographs will also show you what other people see when they look at your model, and you will appreciate your creation through fresh but critical eyes. Photography of models is a long and complex subject, but my experience is that you can do all you want to do indoors with a pair of anglepoise lights with daylight bulbs, which are essentials in a workshop anyway. I never use flash - it is much too harsh for close work, and I do not like being unsure of how a shot will turn out using a flash gun, whereas I can guarantee an image using my incandescent lights. My camera is an old Nikon EL2 which has automatic exposure but is manual in every other way, and that is what you need for this sort of work. All my photos are taken on a boom-armed tripod 'Benbo Trekker' with time exposure using a Tamron 28-50 telephoto lens. I can focus down to 9in in macro mode, or even closer with magnifying lenses, but I seldom use those. Use a fine grain film: ASA100 will give you the crispest shots imaginable; and do not forget to shoot off a roll of colour slides occasionally. You will bless yourself later.

Any model ship over 5ft in length is unlikely to be welcome back in the home, however much you may want to have it displayed in the sitting room, so make sure you have a safe haven in mind for the finished object. Museums, contrary to what you may think, have very little room for large models which are uncommissioned, so do not assume that your masterpiece will be welcomed with open arms, no matter how glorious or wonderful it may be as a finished item. Be aware also that all national museums can only display 10 per cent of what they already possess; the rest

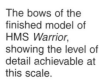

The bows of the finished model of HMS *Warrior*, showing the level of detail achievable at this scale.

of their exhibits are hidden away in warehouses, and sad to say largely unseen.

Large working ship models

Having said all that, I am an unrepentant maker of large, working ship models of a particular sort, which have as their theme auxiliary steam engines assisting the main propulsion of sail. They are all hybrids, where funnels, masts and sails are cheek by jowl, but only one of them can claim to be of warship status.

Since no modelmaker can embrace the whole history of ships, it is a good idea to concentrate on one particular period and work forward from there. It so happens that I have become fascinated by that short period of nautical history spanning the Victorian era, during which sail and steam became a partnership which allowed ships to be more certain of their movements and times of arrival.

My serious modelmaking period began in 1976 with a scratch-built working (steaming) model of the PS Sirius of 1838, the first ships to steam under continuous power from Great Britain to New York; the second was Brunel's Great Britain of 1843,

The wonder of large models. A glimpse through a gunport of a ladderway on the interior of the hull into the secret world below decks (right) and a shot through the stern gallery window (left) showing the full length of the gun deck.

the first screw-propelled ship to cross the Atlantic; and my third was hms Warrior of 1860, the Royal Navy's first iron-built battleship, which can be seen today preserved as a museum in Portsmouth Dockyard and is the subject of this chapter. This was followed by a model of Captain Scott's ship *Discovery* of 1901, one of the last steam-sail hybrid ships.

There is another connecting factor, and that is the Science Museum in London, which carries models of all four vessels in the same scale of 1:48 which I favour. The adoption of this traditional scale for model ships means that all the detail carried on the prototype can be replicated in miniature, and it is still possible (just) to move models of this size to the water's edge, and have them perform in their natural element.

As a child, I felt deep disappointment that the glass case models on show would not be expected to work in water. This careful explanation must have made a deep impression on me, to the extent that the only ship models which I would initially be interested in constructing from scratch in adult life would be fully working models in every sense. In 1974, at age 32, I constructed my first adult model ship from a somewhat altered Billings kit of an ocean-going tug. The alteration was that I wanted it to be powered by steam, and the superstructure had to be built from aluminium in order to disperse the heat,

rather than the hardwood as supplied by the manufacturers. This was half way to scratchbuilding, but I would in hindsight recommend that adult beginners construct their first model from a responsible but not over-fussy kit. Do not go for the *Cutty Sark* or the *Bismarck* as your first choice; skills need to be developed, and everyone needs to learn the trade first. In the initial stages, prepare to be humbled, for there is much to learn and many skills to master, and there is nothing whatsoever wrong with working from a kit.

Early beginnings

When in 1976 my first adult scratchbuilt historical model, the *Sirius*, was coming towards completion, I sent off some photographs to two modelling magazines, one of which showed great interest; John Cundell, the editor of *Model Boats*, asked if I would write up the story from both a historical point of view, and give some constructional details as well, which I was happy to do. This article was published, and it was the beginning of my interest in this period of shipping.

As a next project, the editor asked whether or not I would consider covering the construction of a large model of the *Great Britain*, which at that time was much in the news, having been towed 3500 miles back from the Falklands to the place of her birth in Bristol. This assignment would mean photographing and writing up progress from start to finish, bones, warts and all. It was a daring venture at the time with considerable risks involved from the magazine's point of view. It all took much longer than anticipated, four years rather than two, but the model performed well on the water, and won a gold medal in its class at the Model Engineer Exhibition at Wembley in 1982.

Perhaps the general lesson to be learned from this experience was that you have to double any initially anticipated timescale for projects such as these. So do not agree to finish a model by a deadline unless you are tied into a contract, because you will find you are always behind time, and that is not good for your mental state. Professional modelmakers will always tell you that they could have done more to the finished product, and wanted to do more but the clock beat them. If you are a serious amateur and not ruled by the clock, you ought always to be able to make a better model than a professional who is trying simply to pay the rent and put bread on the table. The amateur is also allowed to keep his model if he wishes, something denied to the professional.

Techniques of hull construction

Although this chapter is about building the hull of my *Warrior* model, the techniques used for building the *Great Britain* model, plank-on-frame with internal eggbox construction, remains an important technique and one which most modellers will follow, so it is briefly described here. The frames were cut from resin-bonded 4mm marine ply, clad with ½in three-ply for the imitation clinchered iron plates. The internal framing was reinforced and waterproofed with a diluted resin paste, and the total hull strongly braced and shielded against boiler heat with an Asbestolux box acting as a coffer-dam amidships. The underside of the decking amidships was also shielded with aluminium, to disperse the generated heat

from a gas burner jet powering the twin cylindered steam engine.

To scratchbuild a large model hull, most modelmakers will initially go for timbered plank-on-frame. It is a strong and reliable method. These days the external planking would normally be backed up with an inner skin of glassfibre tape, or chopped mat strand cloth, resined into place with a stippling brush; alternatively, a loose mix of resin paste can be painted over the total inner area of the hull, or you can employ both paste and glass together. These techniques will produce a strong and stable hull, in which very heavy weights of ballasting, a working model ship with engine/boiler, and other ancillaries like radio control and batteries, will be supported without any flexing of the hull, or effect on propeller shafts or other mechanically moving parts. Plank-on-frame is the strongest and lightest way possible of constructing a vessel, important when you want to put heavy ballast in the right place, and produce a hull which will perform well without the tenderness of topweight. More practically, you only have to make the hull once rather than go through the three-stage process required for moulding.

However, the disadvantage to the plank-on-frame technique in a working model is using an organic material like timber, which wants to shrink and expand in its natural state on a differential basis. It is also difficult to trace where leaks are coming from in an enclosed hull, and over time, when a hull has been exposed to water and strong sunlight, cracks will appear, and water will eventually find its way from the outside to the inside.

The reason so many people nowadays use an ABS preformed hull, or scratchbuild their own from glassfibre, is that a hull produced in a mould will never suffer from seam leakage, and being homogeneous as a material does not wish to swell and shrink like a timber hull. Using a glassfibre technique also means that plating details and so forth on the exterior hull of the ship can be detailed using the original plug from which the mould is to be made. Even the plates themselves, and the rivet lines and items like rigols, can be included if you wish to detail them, and they will be an integral part of the hull, being both strong, realistic and entirely watertight.

The disadvantage of glassfibre hull manufacture is that it involves a three-stage process. You first have to build a plug, around which you make a split mould, and finally you take a moulding from the mould, before you have a model hull to use. It is expensive, time-consuming, and it is much more likely to go wrong on you technically than the conventional plank-on-frame method. If you have no previous experience of work with glassfibre, and no one locally who can help you and assist you, my advice would be to practise on something else first before undertaking a large model ship hull.

Having said that, glassfibre moulding is the way to produce a near perfect and practical hull, and if you are planning on more than one model of the same subject, or even a half-hull to hang on the wall, then be determined and have a go. A good tip would be to try the technique out on, say, the ship's boats, and work up in size to the main hull. Canoe clubs, where they make their own shells, are another possibility, and you would be assured of technical expertise and assistance from those who have made their own canoes on exactly the same principle, though on a marginally larger scale.

The Plug

This is the name given to any object around which a mould is constructed. It is the three-dimensional master pattern used for producing the female mould, and it carries all the detail which will eventually appear on the moulding, the third part of the process. It can be made of any material which has the stability to survive the laying-up process of the mat strand, allowing for the fact that when the curing process is taking place a great deal of heat is produced by the hardener, so any material used must remain stable throughout the process.

The hulls of model boats, particularly larger ones, can be most frugally produced by lath-and-plaster methods for getting the basic shape, and this is what I would recommend. It can also include blocks of hardwood, or softwood, or expanded aluminium mesh, which is good for strange shapes like quarter galleries adopting odd angles. In the case of my *Warrior* model, the lath-and-plaster plug was finished externally with gummed brown paper strip overlaid with draughtsman's tape, impregnated with rivet heads by use of a tailor's wheel making impressions on the sticky side of the tape, prior to being laid over the gummed parcel tape. A whole hotchpotch of materials was then applied just to get detail into the female part of the hull mould. This detail was then replicated when the moulding was laid up inside the mould.

Some books will rather play down the importance of the plug, but I would want to do the opposite. Although it is a sacrificial item, and will be of no further use when the female mould has been produced from it, it is the fundamental object which can save a great deal of time later if it is truly accurate and well finished. You can rely on the outer gel coat, which is the coating making primary contact with the detail on the plug, to reproduce detail faithfully - even down to your thumbprint should you have been unlucky enough to leave it anywhere. It goes almost without saying that smaller models, carved or however produced, can be treated in the same manner; all that is critical is that the pattern is stable.

When the plug has been fully detailed, it has to be slip-waxed and polished with a proprietary potion, so that the laminations of the mould will not stick to the plug. This process is very important, and should be done several times over; a seven-day application is recommended to ensure that the plug cannot under any circumstances weld itself chemically to the mould, or you will be in deep trouble.

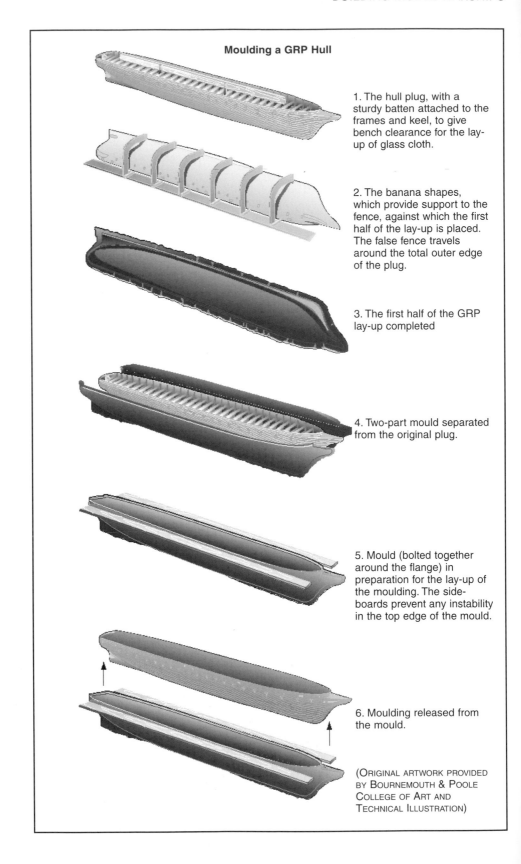

Moulding a GRP Hull

1. The hull plug, with a sturdy batten attached to the frames and keel, to give bench clearance for the lay-up of glass cloth.

2. The banana shapes, which provide support to the fence, against which the first half of the lay-up is placed. The false fence travels around the total outer edge of the plug.

3. The first half of the GRP lay-up completed

4. Two-part mould separated from the original plug.

5. Mould (bolted together around the flange) in preparation for the lay-up of the moulding. The sideboards prevent any instability in the top edge of the mould.

6. Moulding released from the mould.

(ORIGINAL ARTWORK PROVIDED BY BOURNEMOUTH & POOLE COLLEGE OF ART AND TECHNICAL ILLUSTRATION)

Split mould

The second process is making the mould, and because almost all ship hull-forms have what is called undercut, which would prevent them from being able to be released from a conventional open mould, the mould must be made in two separate halves which can be bolted together using an outer flange.

To produce a two-part mould with an integral flange requires a bit of planning and jig-making to lift the plug clear of the building bench by a few inches, and deal with the hull in its inverted state. The need for this clearance is so that the cloth laminations can extend beyond the gunwale or leading edge of the plug for later trimming. Laminators of hulls do not normally lay to a top edge on a boat hull, because the layers of glass cloth can separate on the edge where there is nothing to attach the laminations to - thus the need for this extra inch or so, which can be either filed or cut back when the hull has dried out, or be 'green trimmed' with scissor snips before the layers have fully dried out.

With the hull plug secured to the bench, it is necessary to construct the outer flange through which the retaining bolt holes will be drilled at a later stage. Some banana-shaped timbers need to be cut from plywood. These are secured to the bench and act as a support for the backing timber against which the flange will be laid up. The backing to the flange can be made from any material, allowing for the fact that slip-wax, gel coat and glassfibre mat strand will be laid against it as an integral part of the first half of the mould. The use of plastic parcel tape all over this flange backing will ensure there is no final adhesion from the plug to the mould. The seam between the backing board and the other half of the plug can be sealed successfully with either silicone sealant or Plasticine - anything which will prevent the resin bleeding through to the other side of the plug.

So what you now have is a fully carnuba-waxed and polished plug. At this point most laminators brush or spray on a final coat of PVA (polyvinyl alcohol), which acts as a secondary release agent. With the inverted hull raised above the workbench, your next move is to cover the hull with a pigmented gel coat. This can be

Stern quarter view of the completed hull with deck beams being fitted into the upper deck waterway. Note the use of shower curtains to keep the dust off the model, and increase the light levels.

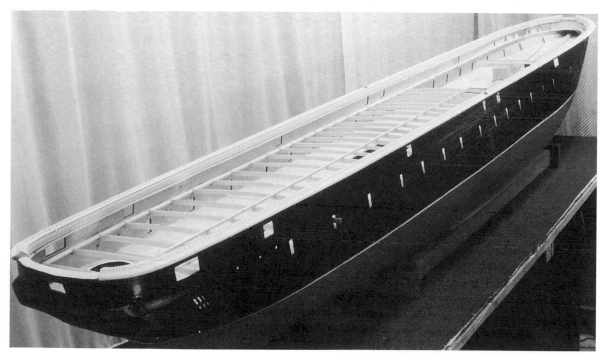

any colour of your choosing, but black is probably going to be your base colour. This pigmented resin is the outer surface of the lamination and it will pick up all the detail of the plug. When two coats of this have cured off you are going to lay up 1½oz chopped mat strand, soaked in resin following the instructions on the tin.

You will need the following items to hand, all available from your nearest glassfibre merchant:

- A tin of thinners for rinsing the stippling brush as you proceed.
- A can for the pigmented resin mix.
- Catalyst bottle, preferably with a calibrated spout.
- A roll of glassfibre tape.

- Large and small brush plus a ribbed roller.
- Scissors suited to cutting the mat strand cloth.
- A weighing machine for the weight of catalyst required.
- Stirring sticks and kitchen roll.
- Bulldog clips and the chopped mat strand cloth cut roughly to size.

If it is your first time, I would suggest you have a helping hand - so that is two face masks, and two pairs of rubber gloves which you will need!

The laminator's job

The trick with glassfibre is to work quickly and efficiently, with everything to hand in the order in which it is going to be required. Technically, the laminator's job is making sure that the cloth is saturated with resin, with no bubbles, creases or trapped air between the layers. You will need a roller as well as a stippling brush so that you can deal with the natural tendency of the cloth to move about. The technique for stippling with the laminating brush is to really soak the cloth, daubing it on rather than brushing it on. If you try to paint it on too neatly you will find that the resin starts to come away with the brush hairs, and a nasty 'hedgehog' starts to form. Keep almost spooning it on with the brush and where necessary rolling it out with a ribbed roller. It is a process which uses a great deal more resin than you would at first suppose, so do not be mean on the proportions of resin when you are mixing it all together. It is not economical to run short halfway through the process.

The false flange running on the top edge of the hull is a useful 'curtain rail' to which clips can be attached to stop the cloth from slipping away in the initial stages. The first application is the most difficult, and that is why you really need a second pair of hands in case of emergencies, particularly with a large area to cover in a short while. It is not difficult, but it does take practice, so do not attempt a large hull

Stern view of the *Warrior* model after deck varnishing.

Figurehead of HMS *Warrior* 1860. Made from a pattern carved in yew, this is a GRP moulding. The torso and arms were separately cast with the Roman shield , a 2-pence coin punched to accommodate the handle.

until your skill levels with this material are up to the task, and never be shy of asking for help and advice locally.

For a large 8ft mould, you will need three layers of 1½oz cloth, and preferably a final finish of a fine woven mat cloth (1oz). This last layer will be much nicer to handle than the rougher textured strand cloth. The reason for the four plies of thickness is that the mould has to be more robust than the subsequent moulding for the purpose of stability and rigidity and manhandling when it comes to the final moment of release from the mould.

Assuming that all has gone well with lay-up of the first half of the mould, complete with its surrounding flange, the false flange and the bananas can be dispensed with, and the Plasticine seal cleaned up, in preparation for the second half to be laid up. This is marginally easier because one is now working without the contrivances of the false flange. There is now a glassfibre flange as an integral part of the first half of the hull, and this can be used to suspend the next layers of cloth, but not before thorough waxing and PVA treatment has taken place along the inside surface of the flange. This is to ensure that the mould will split along its length when it comes time for that to happen.

The four layers of cloth must now be applied to the second half of the plug following the procedures of the first. The plug is now entirely trapped within the envelope of the mould, and must be allowed not only to dry out thoroughly (for at least a week) but also stabilise, so that there is no 'panting' or contortion caused by shrinkage and so forth. The *Warrior* mould was not opened for a full three weeks and has never shown any signs of warping. This is the point where the original plug is dispensed with. It will no doubt suffer in the process of removal but it was always going to be a sacrificial item

Laying up the moulding

Glassfibre is a material which does not mind being applied in patches, which is an odd thing in itself, but provided the gel coat is in place the glass strands will always attach themselves to this outer layer. You would think that it would be necessary to lay down all the glass cloth all at once when laying up a moulding, but this is not the way professional laminators go about it. With something like a mid-Victorian ship's hull there are tight areas at the extremities, such as the galleries at the stern and the trailboards above the stempiece which are both part of the detailed exterior.

The moulding is built up by mat strand glassing these areas first with the mould in two separate halves. Once again, prolific use of the parting agent slip-wax must be applied and polished into the mould, finishing off as before with a coat of PVA. The areas of tight access would be very difficult to lay up if the mould was bolted together, so this is how to overcome that problem; you then join the larger streamlined areas at a later session, building up the layers until the whole of the interior is covered with glass cloth. Two layers of 1½oz mat strand would be adequate, but a third layer using the finer finishing cloth makes the interior of the hull look much tidier.

When you lay up the inside of a hull in a mould, the styrene gas has to be wafted away - literally fanned out of the encapsulated area, because the gas is heavier than air, which will not allow the styrene to cure off unless it is able to escape. Canoe builders invert the hull, literally pouring the gas out as though it were a liquid. Do not use a hairdryer for this - a piece of corrugated cardboard is much more effective.

When the layup is thoroughly dry, the mould will need to be unbolted and split apart with wooden wedges, and this can be a heart-in-mouth job. All your preparations will pay off at this point in terms of the parting agents, but be warned: if you are using a roughened finish the moulding will adhere to the mould like a frightened limpet and will have to be prized apart. Moulds of all sorts improve with further use, and subsequent castings release much more easily.

The released hull moulding will have to be washed down and scrubbed with hot soapy water to get rid of the PVA and the waxy parting agents which will be sticking to the details. The topsides will need trimming down to the top timbers, but the moulding is otherwise ready and waiting for the internal work to begin in the cavernous empty space. A glassfibre hull will not need internal strengthening, but cross beams and decking will obviously brace the midship section where there is no top support, and there will be a need for the addition of risers. These are lining strips

which travel around the inside of the hull and support the deck beams and so forth.

Machinery for boat building

I could easily say that you do not require any machinery, and that it can all be done by hand in the traditional way boats have always been made with hand tools alone. But I love machines, and I am a pragmatist rather than a purist, and if there is a machine tool which will enable me to work with greater accuracy than by hand and eye alone, then I am interested.

Blow lamp and copper tube
We all come to modelmaking from different angles; I used to make musical instruments before I became interested in model ships, so I had the usual hand tools, including a roundfaced spokeshave, which is so useful in shipwrighting, and the luxury of a radial-arm saw and a small bandsaw. I had also developed confidence in bending dampened wood around a heated copper tube when making the ribs of acoustic guitars. This bending jig is a simple device which has multifarious uses in modelmaking, and anybody with a blowlamp can practise the art to their heart's content.

The Vibrosaw
What I did not have was an ability to do mechanically what a coping saw can do: that is to say, cut wood and metal internally. Therefore in the early days I bought an Aeropiccola Vibrosaw; it is now nearly 24 years old and still doing hard work, the original and the best for very fine work - a simple but lovely machine.

Pillar drill
You cannot get far in terms of accurate assembly without the use of a pillar drill. Being fair and square is almost impossible without the guidance which a vertical column brings, and it is a good device for multiple drillings as well. Certain pillar drills with revolving base plates can be

The Aeropiccola Vibrosaw, cutting a hatchway through a removable deckpiece. The blade is so thin it can cut a 90° corner with ease, and no strain - even in metal.

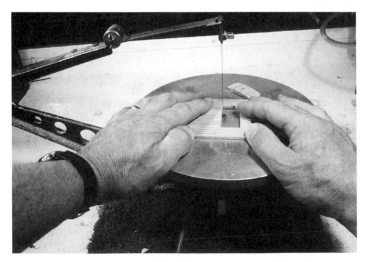

device for the amateur to use. Chisels and small gouges which are so difficult to cope with accurately on a conventional grinding wheel, the spade ends of screwdrivers, plane blades, scalpels, knives, scissors, drill points (with an adaptor), centre punches, scribers . . . and I could go on. Every used tool becomes blunt eventually, and this machine addresses that issue admirably well. Its other great secret is that you can bring the tiniest pieces of stock to the revolving strap, wood, metal or whatever, and machine them without having to clamp them in a pin vice, knowing that the edge is perfectly squared (or angled on the tilting table). The necessity for hand filing is largely removed by this machine, which for the space it occupies is worth its weight in gold.

'Cheap and cheerful' pillar drill *c*1980, using a cross vice for repeat close drilling, measured by the lead screw. Relatively crude in engineering terms, yet very effective.

converted into an indexing machine, which further extends the drill's capabilities. Light milling is possible with the addition of a cross-vice, but this is better done in a dedicated machine as side thrust is not good for the bearings of a pillar drill.

The linisher

If I were starting again, my next buy would be the linisher, which uses a 1in wide revolving belt. This is a machine which holds the key to two vital areas of modelmaking. The first is sharp tools. The linisher is by far the easiest sharpening

Miniature router

I bought a mini router years ago, made by Dremel, whose electrically-powered tools were early in the field of modelling, and particularly respected for their compactness and their power output, being mains-powered. I was impressed by the builder of a full-sized two-seater monoplane who had used one of the early Dremel routers for cutting through the glassfibre panels of his aircraft. It is intended for this kind of work, where chopping with a chisel would shatter the structure and keyhole sawing would be

(left)
The linisher putting a bevel angle on the propeller well cover for the *Warrior* model. This will make a fit like a cork in a bottle.

(below)
Propeller well cover in place, showing the fit achieved by using the linisher. Note the sniping of the planks on the starboard, into the margin plank.

a pain. It is the kind of tool which has endless applications if you can stand the racket and the mess which it causes. I have never yet used it as a spindle moulder, but a table for inverting the tool is now available and would be very useful for making mouldings, etc. Having said that, I have made a personal vow a long time ago never to use a spindle moulder, believing this machine to be inherently too dangerous - the operator is in much more danger than when using a circular saw.

Do I need an engineer's lathe?

Do not imagine that you are the first person to wonder whether or not you can justify buying a lathe. All serious modelmakers toy with this one for ages because it is not only the lathe but also the accessories which are essential if you are going to do anything exciting with the basic machine, apart from just turning bits of wood or metal between centres. The accessories cost about the same amount of money as the basic lathe, so it is a big investment on which you are unlikely to reap your capital outlay.

There are two questions to ask in order to determine the truth about ownership of a lathe. The first question is what can it do for your model boat making? This one is swiftly answered: it will enormously increase your levels of accuracy in terms of handmade fittings which can be made to function mechanically. Second, it will provide the necessary tooling for the intermediate stage of fabrication. For instance, you can make the punch and die of, let us say, a ventilator cowl, which will be subsequently fashioned out of brass sheet. You can also make up the patterns for casting in white-metal and so forth. The more advanced mini-lathes these days carry the option of an overhead, separately-powered miller with a tilting head. This, combined with the accuracy of a lathe cross-slide and the facility of a piece of stock loaded between the headstock and the tailstock, means that the lathe becomes the quintessential manufacturing device.

Everything can be set up for accurate drilling, boring, milling, gear-cutting, dividing, making objects perfectly square, cone-shaped, tapered, threaded internally or externally, and so on. There are great skills involved in the use of a lathe, but the possibilities are all there. You will notice I have not mentioned mastmaking, but this can obviously be done on the lathe, as can all the ancillary fixings like hoops, working sheaves, etc.

The limit of the lathe bed is not so important as you might at first think. You can always join pieces of stock accurately with a lathe, so masts and yards can readily be dowelled or jointed together without any real difficulty. Mini-engineering lathes are also geared by belts to acceptable speeds for woodturning, and present no problem other than the dust they create, dust which, incidentally, ought not to be inhaled by the lathe's motor.

Silver brazing with a propane torch

If you have a lathe you will eventually need to have the facility of joining metal together. Silver brazing is the proper term for hard soldering. You need a propane gas torch to melt silver solder efficiently, and some fire bricks, which will transfer the heat of the flame by reflection and transference to the object being joined. A powdered flux mixed with water is used on the joint, which is brought to red heat to boil the flux. At the moment when it liquefies, a silver-solder stick is applied and as soon as the solder flows the joint is made. This joint will be stronger than the metal itself, and is completely different from soft soldering. Relatively speaking, any amount of pressure may be applied to a silver-brazed joint, and it will not fail.

Casting metal parts in a silicone rubber mould

One of the huge advances in modelmaking comes about from the ability to cast metal items in a silicone rubber mould, the molten metal being a lead/tin mix. Proprietary silicone rubber comes in liquid form in tins with a hardener to cure it off.

All you need is a master-pattern, some Lego bricks for the walls of the mould, some dental plaster for the first half of the mouldmaking process, and some liquid rubber. This rubber can withstand the heat of white metal being poured from a cast iron ladle, so that all kinds of fittings may be replicated - anchors, gun barrels, cleats, and a host of other items which would otherwise take ages to fabricate. The rule for this is: if you have to make more than two identical items, make a mould. It is quicker and much more efficient, and there is something very realistic about a metal casting.

Soft soldering and resistance soldering

There are many instances in modelmaking where silver soldering is not appropriate, and where the total metal surface cannot be brought to a high temperature. Soldering irons then have to be used, with soft solder and flux of the killed salts variety, or multicored in the solder itself. A relatively new mechanism has now appeared on the market called resistance soldering.

This is basically a miniature arc-welding device, using a carbon tip which earths out an electrical charge of high voltage but at low amperage through a dedicated transformer. The carbon tip glows to a high temperature within seconds, and cools down at an equally fast rate. There are several advantages to this system over the more traditional way of soft soldering. First, you can solder very small parts by holding the carbon tip directly onto the piece without the use of clamps when the tip is still cold. You then apply the current, see the previously tinned solder flow, and continue to hold the piece on site with the carbon tip until it cools down. You can then release the pressure and the job will

be done. A conventional soldering iron will not allow you to do this. The electrode heats a small but specific area very quickly, which is what solder likes. This means that other soldered items close by are not affected by the transfer of heat, and do not start coming away as so often happens with conventional irons. Anyone dealing with brass sheet on a more than casual basis might well consider investigating this option, the supplier being Dean Sidings, 41 High Street, Lydney, Gloucestershire GL15 5DD.

The airbrush

If you can possibly afford a small compressor, of the sort dedicated to airbrushing, all your finishing work will benefit enormously. Airbrushing really falls into two categories: general spraying work with an external mix, which is very useful over large areas, and the specifically designed internal mixing airbrush, which will give pencil-thin results, but takes a lot of practice to use to greatest effect. The finish is unquestionably better than brush application, not only because of the ability to apply the paint evenly without brush marks, but also because the jet of air propelling the paint tends to blow away the

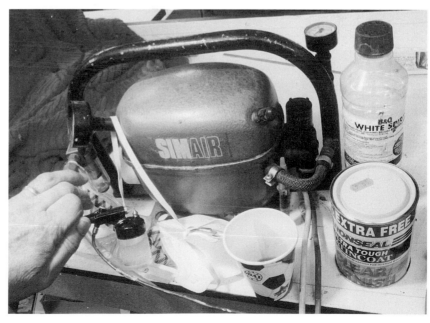

Dedicated airbrush compressor - almost silent in operation.

26   BUILDING MODEL WARSHIPS

minute particles of dust in the area being sprayed. It also assists the drying process. The other great benefit is being able to make invisible repairs, shading colours to match old finishes. If you can manage to afford a compressor, there are a few things to watch out for. Make sure it can cope with at least 40psi - spraying takes about 30psi once the mixture is running nicely, but you need the extra power for some of the larger jobs and thicker paints. It ought to be fitted with a reservoir, and also a blow-down valve for the condensate which accumulates in the air line. The best compressors have no pulse to them as they pressurise a chamber, which acts as a reservoir of air, and this smoothes out the delivery to the jet. Compressors have to be sturdily built, and this accounts for their weight and

price. The last great benefit of a small compressor is ridding models of household dust, particularly useful if you are, for instance, renovating an old model ship which has been uncased for years. Mine has certainly earned its keep over the years.

Metal shearing, bending and punching machine

I mention this machine, which is really a jeweller's item, simply because up until last year, I had no idea such a thing existed. In the world of jewellery, where the metal is very precious, the Swiss produce specialised machines which waste as little as possible of the valuable sheet metal in which they trade. Shearing a piece of metal is infinitely superior to cutting it with snips, or even metal sawing. This is because even strips of, let us say, ½in width, will lie flat when trimmed off the sheet, without any tendency to distortion or curling. It is also excellent for cutting veneers, and can handle repeat requirements of any material likely to be used by a modelmaker. Underneath the guillotine blade lies a second and third option for metal fabrication, a long V-groove which will bend sheet metal to 90° and in a secondary movement fully fold it on the edge if you require. It can also be set up to punch round or square holes up to 12mm with great accuracy. As you would expect, a machine like this which is built to industrial standards is expensive, but might well be infinitely more use than a small lathe. They are about the same price. The name of the supplier is Profiform AG, Udligenswilerstrasse 60, CH-6043 Adligenswill, Switzerland (Telephone 041 370 8850; Fax 041 370 8292).

It is difficult to know where to start and stop with tools. I would just say that the average full sized shipyard has in full scale, examples of everything I have mentioned, and much more besides. Shipbuilding requires all the manufacturing skills known to mankind, so it is hardly surprising that one ends up such a wide assortment of gadgets and gizmos.

The completed 1:48 scale model of HMS *Warrior* at sea in April 1996.
RAY BRIGDEN

2
Waterline Laminated Balsa Models:
HMS *Ocean* 1900

BY ERIC DYKE

MS *Ocean*, the fourth Royal Navy warship to bear that name, was one of six battleships of the *Canopus* class. She was laid down at Devonport Dockyard in 1897, launched on 5 July 1898 and commissioned in 1900. Up to 1903 she was painted in 'Victorian' livery, that is, a black hull with red boot topping that had a narrow white line between the red and the black. She also carried a white or yellow line just below the deck level. Her masts and funnels were buff. In 1903 she was painted overall medium grey, although she did retain her red boot topping for a time. Iron decks were grey, while her wooden decks were scrubbed teak.

The *Ocean* was described as a First Class battleship with a displacement of 12,950 tons (13,360 tons full load).

HMS *Ocean*, a *Canopus* class battleship of 1900, modelled in 1:192 scale by Eric Dyke.

Dimensions: 421ft 6in overall, 74ft beam and 26ft 2in mean depth
Machinery: Greenock Foundry. 20 Belleville boilers, 3-cylinder Triple Expansion engines, two shafts producing 13,500 indicated horsepower, 18.3kts
Armour: Krupps cemented. 6in (152mm) belt, 10-6in (254-152mm) bulkheads, 12in (305mm) conning tower, 2-1in (51-25mm) decks
Armament: 4 x 12in (305mm), 8 x 6in (152mm) QF, 10 x 12pdr QF, 6 x 3pdr QF, 2 Maxim machine-guns, 4 x 18in (457mm) torpedo tubes
Coal bunkerage: 1800 tons. Consumption = 10 tons per hour at full speed
Complement: 682 officers and men

The *Canopus* class were designed for service in the Far East and had somewhat lesser beam and draught than the preceding *Majestic* class on which they were based. The growth of Japanese strength at that time was causing some concern. The displacement some 2000 tons less than the *Majestics* was achieved largely through the use of Krupp armour for the belt and barbettes.

The belt was 6in (152mm) thick which was reckoned to be the equivalent of 8in Harvey nickel armour. This ran for 195ft amidships extending to 5ft below the waterline and 9ft above it. a extension of 2in (51mm) Krupp plating effective only against light shells ran to the bow where it also reinforced the ram. The four 12in guns were mounted in flat-sided twin turrets fore and aft with 8in (203mm) armour on 12in (305mm) armoured barbettes, these reducing to 6in (152mm) inboard of the belt. Eight 6in quick-firing guns were carried at main deck level, the casemates at the ends of the battery being sponsoned out to permit end-on fire. The *Canopus* class were the first battleships to have water tube boilers, which provided the ability to raise steam faster, higher power and better economy at no extra weight, also giving an increase in speed over the *Majestics*.

Ocean had a chapter of accidents during her building, giving her the reputation of being an unlucky ship. Ninety feet of the ship collapsed like a pack of cards when the ribs gave way, and her construction was further delayed by an engineering workers' strike. Furthermore, at her launch on 5 July 1898 she at first refused to move down the slipway and there was a delay of several hours before Princess Louise could complete the launching ceremony, earning the *Ocean* a reputation as the ship that did not want to go to sea. However, she was later one of the first British battleships to pass through the Suez Canal.

On 20 February 1900 the ship was commissioned, proceeding first to the Mediterranean and then to the China Station, where she served until 1905, during which time she was damaged in a typhoon, adding to her reputation as an unlucky ship. She also had several refits. *Ocean* returned from the Far East and paid off into the Chatham reserve, returning to active service with the Channel Fleet in 1906. During 1908 she returned to the Mediterranean, and then joined the Home Fleet on 4 July 1908, where she remained until 1914 when she formed part of the 5th Battle Squadron and sailed to Queenstown. Commanded by Captain Hugo Sadler, she was subsequently employed on protecting convoys in the Persian Gulf, and was then sent to cover the El Shatt operations in January 1915. Then on the 25th of that month she sailed for Tenedos, to take part in the Dardanelles operations, with the battleships *Albion*, *Irresistible*, *Majestic*, *Triumph* and *Vengeance*. On 18 March *Irresistible* struck a mine, and as *Ocean* began to withdraw she too stuck one, and was then hit by a shell which caused flooding in the tiller flat and starboard steering compartment. Irreparably damaged, the ship was abandoned at 19:30, fortunately with all her crew safe, and she sank in Marlo Bay at 22:30 the same night, where she lies to this day. In 2000, the sixth HMS *Ocean* paid tribute to her when she visited the area.

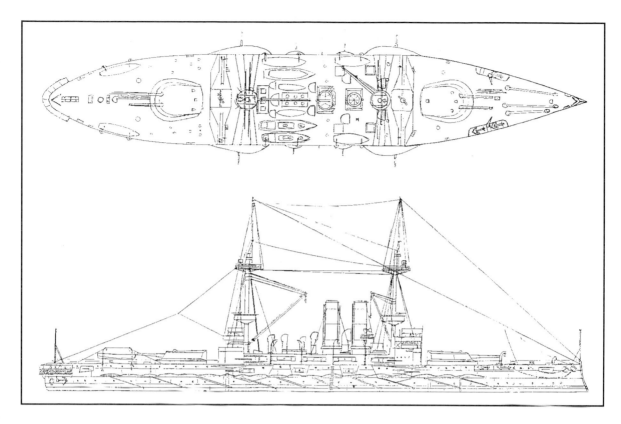

Methods of construction

The model of the *Ocean* was in a way a departure from my usual subjects as it was by far the oldest. I had, however, made models of First World War ships, namely the cruiser HMS *Caroline* and the destroyer HMS *Onslow*. Research did not prove too much of a problem, as I had various books that gave information though I leaned heavily on R A Burt's early battleships book, which as usual with this author was a mine of information for construction of the model.

The model was built to a scale of 1in to 16ft, or 1:192, using my usual method of laminated balsa construction for the hull. At this point I think it would be expedient to explain why I use the materials that I do. Basically the reason is that I am a genuine tabletop modeller, having no workshop facilities nor even any workshop at all!

Tools and materials

Various knives, for example a Swan Moston No 1 Blade craft knife. A tenon saw, a razor saw, various drills mainly used in combination with a pin vice. Wet and dry sandpaper in various grades. A small plane (David) which is of Dutch manufacture that utilises heavy-duty razor blades.

½in Balsa planks. Various thicknesses of plasticard. Glues: usually Evo Stik Extra fast resin, Humbrol Extrabond PVA adhesive, professional polystyrene cement, impact adhesives, Humbrol model filler.

Paints are usually Humbrol which I apply using hand brushes only.

Hull and superstructure

I usually start with the basic hull dimensions, cutting the balsa planks to length and width. I then glue these together (Figure 1). Having waited for the glue to set and harden, I then mark out the plan shape. This encompasses both upper deck and waterline shapes. Before cutting this out I mark the centreline again at waterline and upper deck levels. I repeat the centreline marking at both ends. Then cutting a slot at both ends I insert the pre-shaped elevation

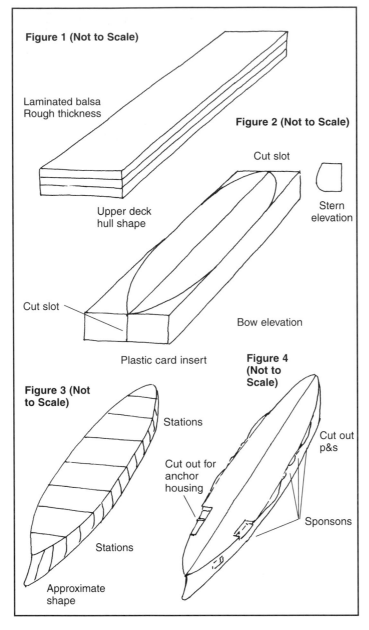

Figure 1 (Not to Scale)

Laminated balsa
Rough thickness

Upper deck
hull shape

Cut slot

Figure 2 (Not to Scale)

Cut slot

Stern
elevation

Bow elevation

Plastic card insert

**Figure 3 (Not
to Scale)**

Stations

Cut out for
anchor
housing

Stations

Approximate
shape

**Figure 4
(Not to
Scale)**

Cut out
p&s

Sponsons

view in plasticard (Figure 2). This enables
me to get bow and stern in line to shape
without constant checking, making the
whole procedure rather easy. I then cut the
shape of the upper deck (Figure 3), then
begin to shape the hull working down to
the waterline, using templates at various
stations to check the shape. I then work on
the sheerline. Although it is not so
pronounced it still exists on the *Ocean*.
This gives a fairly accurate shape. Before
plating there are various cutouts in the hull
for forward and aft-facing guns (Figure 4).
Again there are the 6in gun sponsons fore
and aft. These also require cutouts before
fitting. I found it expedient to actually fit
the guns and mounting details, *ie*
armoured doors, before attaching them to
the hull sides. The last hull requirement
was to cut out the anchor recesses. Because
the ship had three anchors, the cutout on
the port side was consequently smaller
than that on the port side. I then plated the
hull with the cut plasticard, usually in ⅓in
by 3in strips, starting at the starboard bow
and working back (Figure 5). Having
completed the hull plating I bored holes
for the scuttles and the lower parts of the
torpedo netting booms. Because of the
black-painted hull I found it necessary to
press grey plastic discs to give background
to the old X-ray film that I use to simulate
glass to give it extra sparkle, then giving
the scuttles a coat of clear varnish.

At first glance, the superstructure of
Ocean looked easier to make than that of
more modern vessels, but the need to
accommodate the 6in battery either side

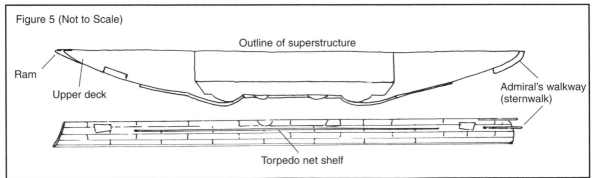

Figure 5 (Not to Scale)

Ram

Upper deck

Outline of superstructure

Admiral's walkway
(sternwalk)

Torpedo net shelf

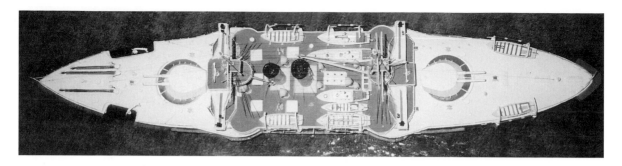

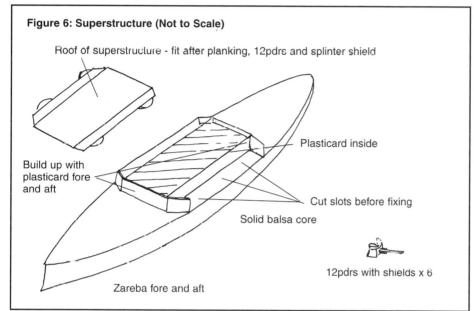

Figure 6: Superstructure (Not to Scale)

Roof of superstructure - fit after planking, 12pdrs and splinter shield

Plasticard inside

Build up with plasticard fore and aft

Cut slots before fixing

Solid balsa core

12pdrs with shields x 6

Zareba fore and aft

Overhead view of the model, showing the shape of the hull, the cutouts for the anchors (forward) and the sponsoned-out casemates at each end of the superstructure to allow end-on fire for the 6in guns.

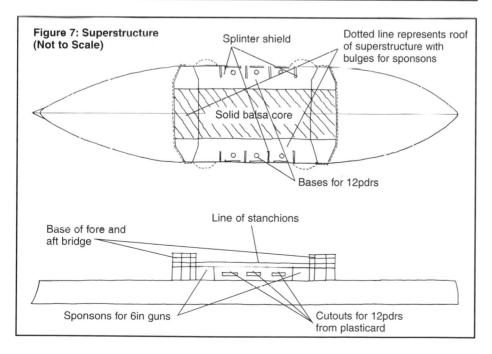

Figure 7: Superstructure (Not to Scale)

Splinter shield

Dotted line represents roof of superstructure with bulges for sponsons

Solid balsa core

Bases for 12pdrs

Line of stanchions

Base of fore and aft bridge

Sponsons for 6in guns

Cutouts for 12pdrs from plasticard

meant that it had to be built up. A piece of plasticard measured to fit the required length and width formed the base on which to build the superstructure itself. I then plated a central block fore and aft then fitted it to the base. I then took a thicker piece of plasticard, measured and cut out the slots for the three broadside guns on each side and then fitted it to the outside edge. When dry I reinforced the plating between each slot, which also served to simulate the armour between each gun position. There would also have been armour plate in inverted 'V' shapes behind each gun, but this would not be visible on the completed model so did not require to be built.

The next job was to replicate the base of the superstructure unit to serve as its upper deck. When this was fitted the ends were plated in, the plating behind extended upwards at each end to provide a zareba around the conning towers, which were themselves built using the standard balsa and card method from suitably sized pieces of dowling. The sighting ports were cut in using the same measuring method as on the gun turrets, and the slightly domed roofs of the towers were constructed by fitting a suitably-sized plasticard disc and sanding it into shape in *situ*, after which the towers were fixed in place.

Then came the bridge and the bridge wings, which had to be built out on stanchions over the conning towers. Again the bridge was built up on a base that formed its floor, but before building the sides and bulwarks, the interior details such as the Pelorus compass and ship's wheel first had to be built, painted and fitted. The bridge walls were then built up. These having many windows, I employed my 'cover and cut' method. Simply make a strip of plastic just under the required size of the windows, glue to the sides of the bridge, allow to dry and then just cut round them to make the windows. As the sides of the bridge were open to the elements, the necessary cut-outs had to be made. Then all four sides were fitted and glued. The bridge wings had steel railings and to simulate the canvas 'dodgers' I took good-quality tissue paper (of the type that comes in shoe boxes), glued this to the rails and gave it a coat of sanding sealer before painting. The bridge roof is then cut out, with railings around the top built in the same way as those on the bridge wings. Once dry, and after the inside of the bridge has been painted (varnished teak, otherwise white) the roof is glued in place. An interesting thing was that on most RN battleships of this period the bridge searchlights were mounted on a track. This may have been to give them some protection from the elements. I cannot think of any other reason! Also, there were semaphore arms on each bridge wing.

The ventilators were a very noticeable feature of warships of this period after forced-draught ventilation had been introduced in the *Duncan* class battleships. Taking suitably-sized plastic tube cut to the required length, I scallop one end to receive the bowl of the ventilator, which is made in the same way as the boat

Close-up of the midships section of the model.

funnels, that is by using a male and female mould. Using plastic rods of various thicknesses I shape the ends to create a dome shape. Because of the larger size of these pieces I use any available form of plaster to create the female mould. When set but not dry, press the rod into the plaster and then leave for 48 hours. Then heat thin pieces of plasticard over a flame and press them into the mould with a rod to form the bowl shapes. These are then glued to the scalloped end of the plastic tube. After drying put plastic padding around the result, then smooth to shape with wet and dry sandpaper. Fit the prominent turning boards around the tube upright, then drill out the opening in the bowl with a hand drill or a pin vice drill. How often have I judged models at competitions which had solid ventilator bowls! The above method allows a proper appearance to be given relatively simply. A plastic disc of appropriate size is then fitted at the other end to give good adhesion to the deck. Finally, a cross-shaped guard was fitted over the opening of the bowl, as was the practice on the original *Ocean*.

The funnels were constructed from balsa cores with plasticard bent around

them in upright strakes, giving a certain amount of depth to the inside of the funnel without losing strength.

The lower sections of the masts, which are tapered, were made by simply using suitably-sized old paintbrushes, while the yards and topmasts were made from dowling. The circular fighting tops, which mount 3pdr guns, were made of discs of plasticard with a central hole for the mast. Stuck at the right height up the mast, the undersides were built up with balsa and plasticard to give the taper, with the coaming built up around this. The boat derricks and booms on the masts were again built up from dowling.

Armament
As with most RN battleships of this period, *Ocean*'s main armament consisted of two twin 12in turrets. The model's turrets were constructed using the same method as the hull and superstructure, first cutting and masking the basic shape from solid balsa. The turrets of the *Canopus* class were rather complicated in shape and I found it easier to construct them in two pieces, an upper half and a lower half. The lower half was the barbette which projected above the

The forward 12in turret of *Ocean*. The different shapes of the gunhouse and the barbette it stands on can clearly be seen.

upper deck, an oval shape which was more bevelled aft than forward, and the upper half was the gun-house itself, also a complicated shape as it had a pronounced sloped roof and sides, obviously intended to help deflect shells. After making the basic shapes, I plated them with Plasticard. This had to be done in segments with any gaps or joints filled with plastic padding and then sanded. The turrets were then set aside for the moment.

The gun barrels were the next item. As a table-top modeller, my method for this differs from that of others. Starting with a piece of suitably-sized plastic rod, I mark the required length of the barrel on it but I do not at this stage cut the rod to size, using the rest of it as a hand-hold while I turn the rod and shape it with a sharp knife (Swan Morstan Blade No. 1), finishing off with wet and dry sandpaper.

To fit the guns into the turrets I first mark the slots to receive the barrels and mantelets by simply cutting thin pieces of plasticard, attach them to the face and top of the turret according to the plan, and then

cutting around them when they are thoroughly dry. Simple but effective. Be sure to measure the inside to ensure that the result is the right size. Removing the plastic, cut a slot in the balsa core and line it with Plasticard to receive both barrel and mantelet. The gun mantelet is made using discs of laminated plastic to fit into the slots. These are then cut across and the resulting half-discs faced with thin Plasticard. To give a smooth finish I then drill a ⅛in hole to receive the gun barrel. I then cut the barrel from the rod, allowing an extra ¼in to cut the end to fit the hole in the mantelet. This is then glued into the turret, and details such as sighting hoods, etc, are added to the turret roof.

The other guns were fitted either in casemates or on the superstructure. The casemates at the four corners of the superstructure allowed their 6in guns a theoretical 180°, permitting end-on fire fore and aft. There were four other casemates along the sides. All these were built in the usual way, ie balsa core and plasticard plating. Slots were cut into them

The seconday armament - 6in guns in casemates at the corners of the superstructure and 12pdrs along the sides.

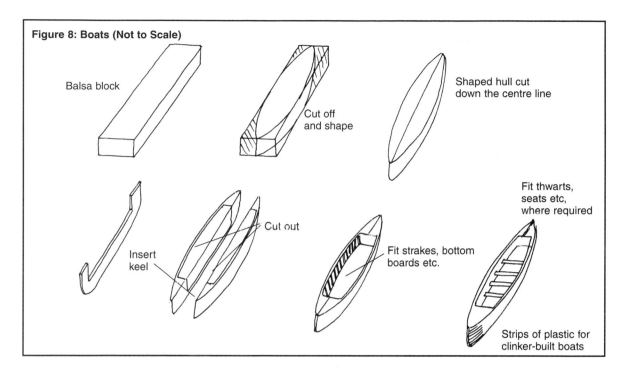

Figure 8: Boats (Not to Scale)

Balsa block

Cut off and shape

Shaped hull cut down the centre line

Insert keel

Cut out

Fit strakes, bottom boards etc.

Fit thwarts, seats etc, where required

Strips of plastic for clinker-built boats

for the guns and armoured doors fitted in the open position. The guns were made in the same way as the turret guns, but in this case the mantelets were placed on their sides to simulate the armoured shields. The 6in guns in the open casemates and the 12pdrs on the superstructure were built with full detail, breeches, trunnions etc, but only the barrels were fitted to the closed casemates. The 3pdrs on the fighting tops likewise had to be fully detailed, but since many of these were later used as saluting guns the information was easy to find. I was unable to find any details on the position and type of Maxim machine guns carried. They had replaced earlier 0.5in calibre Nordenfeldt guns on mobile mountings, so may have been similar.

The battleships of this period all carried anti-torpedo netting which is simulated on the model by using tissue as the netting covers.

Boats

The *Ocean* normally carried twelve boats:

One 50ft steam pinnace, which doubled as a gunboat with either a 3pdr or a 0.5in Maxim machine gun.
One 40ft Admiral's barge with armament as above.
One 45ft steam pinnace with armament as above.
A 42ft sailing launch.
Two 36ft sailing pinnaces.
Two 32ft cutters.
One 32ft galley.
Two 27ft whalers.
One 16ft dinghy.

Ocean's three steam pinnaces were modelled as follows. Blocks were cut from balsa wood to the outside dimensions, masked to plan and elevation and then cut and sanded to shape. The boat was then cut in half lengthways. One half was then placed on a piece of plasticard and the profile shape of the keel cut out. I then attached the other half. Over the next 48 hours I painted the resulting shape with sanding sealer, sanding between each coat. The next stage was to make any cutouts, attach the decking and build the superstructure. The steam pinnaces had fore and aft decking, and the small scuttles were made by cutting short lengths of fine

The boat deck of *Ocean*. Note the detailing inside the ship's boats, the classically-shaped ventilators, the 3pdr guns in the fighting tops and the semaphore arms at the ends of the bridge wings.

plastic tube, and blocking in the results with matt black paint followed by a coat of clear gloss. The outside part of the scuttle was made by simulating brass with gold paint on the rim of the tube - it looks very effective! The brass funnels were simply the same kind of tube with a disc of plastic at the end. After drying this disc was drilled out to the inside character of the funnel, then using a small amount of plastic padding under the rim of the resulting funnel which, after hardening, was sanded to a reverse-bell shape. The ventilators were made by making a male shape from a plastic rod which was used to shape a female balsa mould, then heating some thin Plasticard and pressing out the bell of the ventilator which was then attached to a thin piece of plastic rod. Again very effective!

The same procedure was basically used for building the other boats, but there are differences in detail when constructing open boats. Carvel-built boats have to be

given a smooth surface. Before attaching the keel both sides were partly carved out, not completed but enough to be attached to the keel. When dry, finish carving the inside, again after using the Sanding Sealer to firm up the outside, and attach thwarts, strakes etc, to the inside, not forgetting the keel board box that was a prominent feature of all boats designed to carry sails. Any seats can then be attached, together with rowlocks, cleats etc, and then outside details such as rubbing strakes, safety lines, rudders and propellers if required.

Clinker-built boats are more complicated, as they have to have overlapping external planking. The beauty of using plastic card is its flexibility. The planking is built up from strips of plastic card cut to size and laid one on top of the other, working from the top down. I have learnt the hard way that it is advisable to do the outside planking before finishing the inside carving! After allowing the outside to harden, fit the accoutrements as above. To give an added touch of accuracy I sometimes lay the rudder inside the boat, not on the pintles, as per RN practice.

Methods of painting boats are very much an individual thing. However, if a model is being painted in contrasting colours, a straight line is needed and this is best achieved by using cut-down Tamiya masking tape, which is very good stuff.

The model of *Ocean* was built in ten weeks, firstly as a subject for this article, and secondly to loan to the LPH HMS *Ocean* where it now resides with a model of the sixth *Ocean*. I do hope that this chapter gives some idea of the methods that I have developed over the years to create a relatively inexpensive form of model ship construction. As a final word, it cannot be stressed too much that it is vital to thoroughly research the subject modelled.

I would like to thank the Commanding Officers of HMS *Ocean* (L12) Captain (now Rear-Admiral) Scott Lidbetter and Captain Adrian Johns, for their help and encouragement with both of the *Ocean* models and their permission to use the commissioning book that proved of great help. Also Mr John Linwood for help with the photography.

3
Modelling an Inter-War Aircraft Carrier:
HMS *Glorious* 1936

BY BRIAN KING

At the outbreak of the Second World War the big-gun battleship was seen as the capital ship of the world's navies, but by the end of that catastrophe its position had been usurped by the aircraft carrier. The battleship had become more of a liability in need of protection. Even the mighty Japanese battleships *Yamato* and her sister ship, *Musashi*, were sunk by air power, their 18in guns and superior optics being of no use with no surface target in range. During the war in the Pacific large battles were fought between fleets that were never in visual contact, the damage being inflicted by their air arms operating from large fleet aircraft carriers. Launching air reconnaissance followed by strikes far beyond the big gun's reach, the most important ships in the fleet became the carriers.

Before 1914, the Royal Navy experimented with float planes (typically Short Type S38), both taking off from the water and from specially constructed ramps built on the forward turrets of the warships *Hibernia* and *London*. Successful take-offs were achieved with the ships steaming at 10-12kts into the wind, the aircraft then landing on the water. Even attempts at wireless communication were carried out at this time. It was also apparent that wheeled aircraft had a better performance than seaplanes but these required solid surfaces for take-off and landing.

During the First World War seaplane carriers were used as motherships carrying supplies and hangars for their broods. HMS *Engadine* was actually with Beatty's Battle Cruiser Fleet at Jutland as was *Campania* which was carrying seven single-seater fighters for defence and three wireless-equipped Short 184 aircraft for reconnaissance. But *Campania* was ordered back to port early on and *Engadine*'s part in the battle was limited. The truth was that airframe strength, engine reliability and wireless equipment development were all wanting at this time but from these small achievements such successful air strikes as Taranto and Midway were the eventual outcome.

The years between the World Wars were difficult times of financial stringency for all navies, but experiments to refine the ship/aircraft combination continued, albeit at a slower pace. Up until then partially flight-decked vessels had been used with sometimes-fatal attempts to land aircraft onto limited deck areas. The history of the development of the aircraft carrier to its final form, *ie* a full-length flat flight deck, can be seen in the development of one ship, HMS *Furious*, a 'light' battlecruiser. (How a ship carrying two 18in guns, one forward and one aft, can be called 'light' is another story.) Her first refit saw the removal of the forward 18in gun and the building of a hangar large enough for ten aircraft. The top was extended to the bows to act as a flying-off deck 228ft long and 50ft wide.

Normally the wheeled aircraft landed on the sea, being kept afloat by airbags until they were hoisted inboard. Obviously to land-on would require flying aircraft alongside the superstructure and then to sideslip onto the deck around the bridge works, which was thought impossible. However, Squadron Commander E H Dunning thought otherwise and, on 2 August 1917, succeeded in landing-on with the ship underway – the first time this had been done. Further attempts were stopped when Dunning, brave man he, was killed on his third attempt five days later.

It was obvious that what was required was a landing-on deck aft, so the after gun and main mast were removed between November 1917 and March 1918

and a hangar was built with a flight deck on top measuring 284ft long and 70ft wide. Lifts to the hangars below were installed on both fore and aft decks. In addition decks were arranged on each side, around the remaining superstructure, to connect the fore and aft decks for aircraft movements. Total capacity was increased to sixteen wheeled aircraft.

The recurring arrester problem was tackled by fitting fore and aft wires 9in above deck level. Transverse ropes with attached sand bags each end were laid on these wires. Forward of these an upwards-sloping ramp was built. The aircraft, single-seater Sopwith Pups, were fitted with skids and hooks to engage the transverse ropes. The final safety feature was a rope barrier to

Brian King's model of HMS *Glorious* as in 1936, with her complement of aircraft, in 1:192 scale.

stop a aircraft from crashing into the remaining central superstructure if it had not been stopped by either the ropes or the ramp. This landing-on deck was not successful owing to the turbulence created by the remaining superstructure, which was made worse by the hot furnace gases emerging from the funnel which was, of course, still on the ship's centreline.

The final refit saw *Furious* converted to a totally flush-decked ship. The furnace gases were discharged from vents along the sides aft, following the recently-completed *Argus* whose design had, in turn, been greatly influenced by the difficulties experienced with the superstructure on *Furious*. *Argus* had been a partly-built Italian passenger ship taken over and converted to become the world's first flush-decked carrier with a speed of 19kts and a below-decks hangar capable of holding up to twenty aircraft.

Experiments were carried out on *Argus* to solve the difficult problem of decelerating aircraft on landing. Aircraft at this time had no brakes. Arrester wires running along the deck were first tried. These were 300ft long and were hopefully engaged by 'V' shaped hooks on the under carriage of the landing aircraft. Palisades were fitted to prevent aircraft from falling over the side. Safety trip wires were installed at the deck edges and if the aircraft touched these the powered palisades were raised automatically. However, this arrangement of arrester wires was not the final answer.

Following *Furious*, *Eagle* and *Hermes* were commissioned. *Eagle* had been laid down initially as a Chilean battleship but *Hermes* was the first ship designed from scratch as an aircraft carrier. She carried an 'island' superstructure with a funnel on the starboard side of the flight deck and this feature has become standard on most carriers ever since.

Development of *Glorious*

Courageous, *Glorious* and *Furious* were three 'light' battlecruisers which had become white elephants. They had been built for Admiral Fisher's proposed Baltic operations but these had never come to anything. Their light armour and small number of heavy guns made them unsuitable for fleet operations but their length and high speed made them prime candidates for conversion to aircraft carriers.

Following the work on *Furious*, *Courageous* and *Glorious* were stripped to main deck level and rebuilt with a main flight deck that stopped short of the bows. There was a secondary short flight deck at main deck level which enabled lightly wing-loaded aircraft, such as the delightful Fairey Flycatcher fighter, to take off directly out of the lower hangar. This aircraft was the last to be able to do this; subsequent aircraft with a higher wing loading were not able to get airborne on such a restricted run. All future carriers had the flight deck taken to the bows as exemplified by the *Ark Royal* of 1937.

Building the Model

My family and I, as a small boy of ten, spent a summer holiday in Portsmouth during Navy Week in 1935. We took a boat trip around the harbour to see, among others, the aircraft carrier *Courageous* alongside. The other ships, I remember were the 'mighty 'ood' (HMS *Hood*) and *Nelson*, some of which, including *Courageous*, unhappily did not survive the coming war. It was this visit that persuaded me to build a carrier as a change from battleships, my usual choice. These two carriers, *Courageous* and *Glorious*, were very interesting ships visually as they were more 'fussy' than the later, more streamlined *Ark Royal*.

In the event I chose to build her sister-ship *Glorious* as, in 1936, she had had her flying deck lengthened at the aft end. It was supported by four large struts in the form of a large 'W' which made her even better looking. I obtained 'as fitted' plans from the National Maritime Museum, after initially being told none were available,

although a general view of the port side was missing. This had to be made up from examination of the appropriate deck plans. These plans were reduced to a scale of 1:192 which would make a decent-sized model for display but not too big for handling. A list of MOD drawings used is in the Sources.

Photographs, an essential tool for the modeller, came next. I went down to Yeovilton to the Fleet Air Arm Museum to examine their photo collection which, for one reason or another, was not very helpful – blurred pictures, etc. But Wright and Logan of Portsmouth (sadly no longer in business) did supply some good shots that were most helpful including three photos of the elusive port side. While both sides of most naval vessels are similar, this does not apply to carriers.

The next step was to decide at what period should the model show the ship. This would affect the type of aircraft carried etc. I decided on 1936 – the time of the Spanish Civil War – when 'foreign' ships operating in the area had to display their nationality. This was done on *Glorious* with a rectangle of red, white and blue on the flight deck. It also meant models of Blackburn Baffins (two-seat torpedo bombers), Fairey Seals (three-seat spotter bombers), Hawker Ospreys (two-seat fighters) and Hawker Nimrods (single-seat fighters) would be on board. Note, all these are canvas-covered biplanes - real aeroplanes (in the writer's eyes) not modern metal aircraft! Although I love

aircraft as much as ships, modelling them presents new difficulties. Their 'square' shape just does not sit on the mantelpiece as well as ships. In this case, however, owing to their size, this problem did not exist! I eventually made twenty-four planes but more of this later.

Having decided on the above, it had to be decided how the model was to be built, as it posed problems not encountered before.

The hull

The hull up to the main deck was no real problem: a lot of hard carving work but all familiar stuff. The lift system (bread-and-butter) was adopted, using jelutong as the timber. The main problem was that the anti-torpedo bulge was elliptical in shape (in side view) and the thickness of the lifts selected had to take this into account. Waterlines were redrawn where necessary to accommodate the lift thickness. It is essential to let your timber supplier know that the thickness of these lifts is very important if you buy PAR (planed all round) material. I once had a series of about six lifts all come out 1mm too thin. Six times 1mm is ¼in, which played havoc with the assembly. It was obvious that the planing machine was set wrongly and nobody had bothered to check it.

Figure 1 is a copy of my working drawing of the transverse sections. The 'difficult to build' anti-torpedo bulge can be seen – quite a nightmare to make. It can also be seen that only four lifts were used:

The four types of aircraft made for the model. From left to right, the Fairey Seal, the Hawker Osprey, the Blackburn Baffin and the Hawker Nimrod.

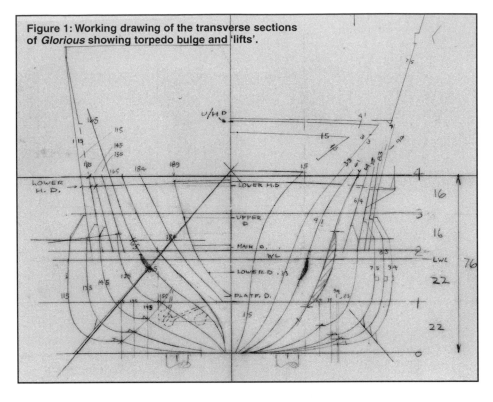

Figure 1: Working drawing of the transverse sections of *Glorious* showing torpedo bulge and 'lifts'.

two of 22mm and two of 16mm giving a total depth of 76mm. Each lift was made of two pieces with the joint vertical on the keel centreline. This is to enable the centres of the lifts to be band-sawed out. Even the 'solid' bottom lift is made in two pieces thus giving a glued-in centreline which will remain, however much material is removed, unlike pencil lines that disappear with the first plane stroke.

The real problem was how to make the superstructure above the main deck.

Briefly this consisted of two main layers: the lower hangar whose deck was at main deck level and the upper hangar above with the flight deck itself acting as its deck head. Seen in section, these form two long boxes whose sides consisted of vertical fore and aft bulkheads running parallel to the keel line for most of the ship's length. Figure 2 shows a typical transverse arrangement. Not only can the hangars be seen but also the two semi-triangular areas at either side. In general the part marked 'A' was enclosed

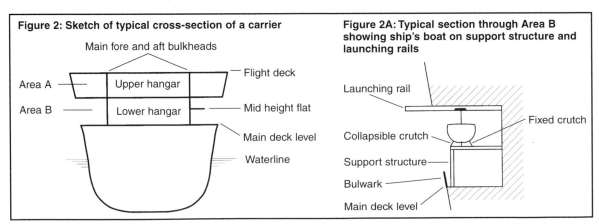

Figure 2: Sketch of typical cross-section of a carrier

- Main fore and aft bulkheads
- Flight deck
- Area A — Upper hangar
- Area B — Lower hangar
- Mid height flat
- Main deck level
- Waterline

Figure 2A: Typical section through Area B showing ship's boat on support structure and launching rails

- Launching rail
- Fixed crutch
- Collapsible crutch
- Support structure
- Bulwark
- Main deck level

except for ports but the area 'B' was largely open and housed guns (4.7in QF Mark VIII on the HLA XII mounting) or ship's boats. In addition most of these areas also had a mid-height flat over some of their width, housing winches, urinals, etc. These flats were fully detailed on the model including the necessary guardrails. Unfortunately, on completion all this detail was almost completely hidden by ship's boats, etc. much to my annoyance. It was found desirable to produce rough free-hand sketches of the layouts in the embrasures to get the feel of the job and to visualise what was required (see Figure 3).

Incidentally, the ship's boats were hung from twin horizontal rails, which projected beyond the ship's side for launching. Orthodox davits were of course not possible. To allow these boats to be moved sideways out of the embrasures the outer half of their crutches were hinged flat. They could not be lifted vertically out of their crutches in the normal manner owing to the deck head of the embrasure. The only two boats (one each side) not in embrasures were the RAF 37ft 6in seaplane tenders housed on sponsons at the rear of the superstructure (see photograph). It must be remembered that the RAF and not the Navy were responsible for the aircraft on naval ships up to May 1939 when full

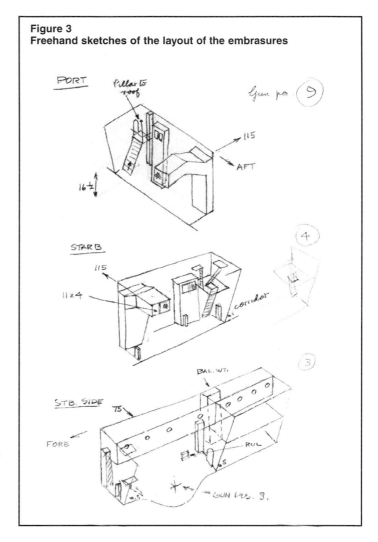

Figure 3
Freehand sketches of the layout of the embrasures

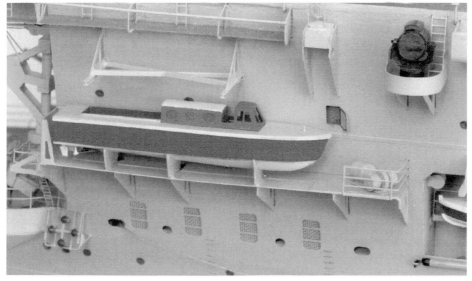

RAF 37ft 6in seaplane tender on sponsons aft.

control of the Fleet Air Arm (FAA) finally returned to the Admiralty. This dual control, with the RAF not being overly concerned with naval matters, resulted in naval aircraft lagging behind although the Swordfish torpedo bomber did a rather good job, even outliving its replacements!

The horizontal members, lower hangar deck head and flight deck were made of plywood. The vertical bulkheads were of ply and bass wood (American Lime) where thicker material could be fitted. Where possible balsa packing blocks were used. For instance, most of the areas marked 'A' were so fitted. Balsa, a material which I normally never use as it is too soft, was used because the outside needed to be shaped and cleaned up and by using balsa this could be done with minimum force, the whole superstructure being a bit flimsy

at this stage. The balsa also provided a gluing surface for the subsequent plating. Internal access was necessary throughout the building programme so the lower hangar was fixed to the main deck and the upper hangar, including the flight deck, kept as a separate but easily assembled and disassembled piece. The photograph shows the three units before assembly. In the middle is the hull up to main deck level, below is the lower hangar and above the upper hangar and flight deck. The next photograph shows the fixing of the lower hangar to the hull.

The outside hull face, that is from main deck to flight deck, presented a problem. What to make it from? I decided that it might be possible to make it of metal – brass for instance. Except in two places, the surface was a vertical sloping straight

Unassembled hull (centre), flight deck and upper hangar (top), lower hangar (bottom).

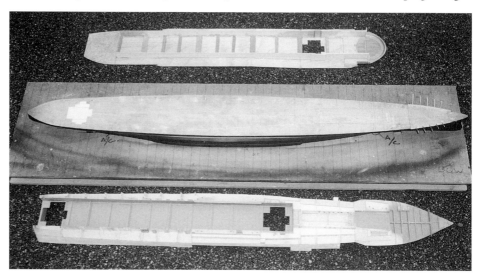

The assembly of the lower hangar to the main deck.

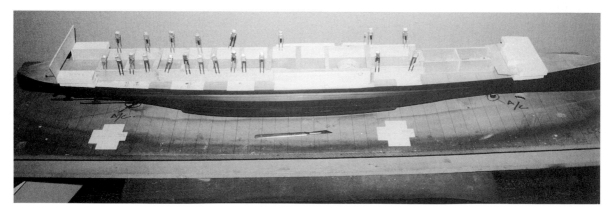

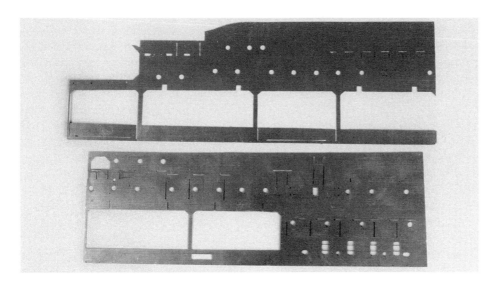

Two etched hull plates in 0.008in brass.

line. Its slope varied along the hull but at every vertical section it was a straight line. Therefore, flat plate or plates could be used except in the two places mentioned. Having checked the facts, as it were, it was decided to 'plate' this area with 0.008in etched brass shim. This would enable really crisp detailing to be achieved – all holes, ports etc, being etched in before assembly. It also allowed scale thickness to show around the embrasures etc. There were, however, two minor problem – one was possible trouble due to the differing coefficients of expansion of wood and brass breaking the glue line and, secondly, what glue to use to accommodate the first problem. A few calculations indicated that a length of 7in should not incur any excessive stretching of the glue line so the plates were made 7in long. What was also wanted was a flexible glue that did not go off completely. This was solved by using R/C Modellers Craft Glue which, in fact, does not set hard and dries transparent. It is never a good idea to glue long lengths of different materials together because of the stress induced in the glue line by temperature variations. Short lengths yes but long ones no!

To obtain the drawings for the photo-etching process, thin card was attached to the hull sides and held in place with pins. The required holes, apertures,

etc. were then drawn on using the baseboard as a datum. It must be appreciated that as the vertical slope varied along the card's length it was in effect twisted so visually straight lines were slightly curved when the cards were removed and flattened. At this stage they were traced off onto tracing film. It was, at that time, usual to make the etching drawings twice full size to improve accuracy and to sharpen up the image. It was decided that increasing the size by photocopying would be liable to introduce distortion errors so they were left actual size. I say 'at that time' as most etching drawings of mine are now computer derived and, because of the accuracy, are drawn to size. The photograph shows two etched hull side plates.

Photo etching

All the above assumes that the reader is familiar with the photo-etching process. For those unfamiliar with the system it uses ferric chloride as an etching medium to etch out parts from brass (or other metal) sheet. A drawing is required to enable 'acetates' to be made. These are the masks that allow the design to be transferred to a light-sensitive emulsion covering the metal sheet. After exposure to UV light to develop the image, areas of the emulsion can be washed off, exposing the metal to allow the etchant to attack the sheet. The whole process can be done at home using printed circuit board (PCB) equipment available from suppliers such as Maplins, but I always produce the drawings but get the actual etching done by professionals who have far better equipment than I can afford. The process is akin to PCBs but these have a plastic backing sheet of course. For further details see the book *Photo Etching* by the author of this chapter and Azien Watkin. Photo etching can be used for all sorts of parts and great use of the process was made in the detailing of the fittings required in the building of this vessel.

The Island

This and the funnel were made from Perspex sheet and tube (see photograph). There was nothing very difficult here except the design of the bridge structure required some sorting out. One blurred aerial picture rather indicated that further work had been done on the bridge area sometime after 1936 but no firm information could be found. The island was an interesting structure on several counts. It had an air bridge that could be swung out over the flight deck like a cantilever and swung back and stowed alongside the base of the funnel. This feature was not repeated on

subsequent carriers as far as the writer is aware. The bridge area was also festooned with voicepipes, unusually fitted on the outside, which made a nice feature.

Ship's Boats

These comprised the two RAF tenders already mentioned and the following:

    2 x 36ft motor pinnaces
    2 x 35ft crash boats
    1 x 32ft motor cutter (port side only)
    2 x 32ft pulling cutters
    1 x 30ft cutter (starboard side only)
    2 x 30ft gigs
    2 x 27ft whalers
    2 x 16ft dinghies

Details of these boats were found in various ship Anatomy books. The only trouble with this is that basically they are all the same drawings. One would like to see a little variety in these boat drawings. All the models were made in the traditional way using heated polycard and a plug and die to produce the moulded shells. The plug needs to be the same shape as the interior of the boat whereas the die only needs to be a plan-shaped hole with its top edge rounded to allow the polycard to flow into the cavity as the plug is forced in. There are several points to watch with this moulding process. The forefoot of the moulding can often become very thin due to excessive stretching. The cure for this is either to use thicker sheet or to reinforce this area with some paste. If the shells are made of ABS, Isopon (polyester paste) can be used, whereas if they are made of polycard you will need to use Milliput (epoxy paste), as Isopon will not adhere very satisfactorily to polystyrene. The

The unpainted funnel and island made from Perspex, brass and aluminium.

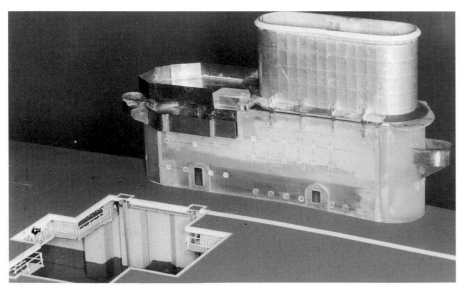

other problem is that because the die is not of full form, any concave curves will not be reproduced, as the material will simply stretch over any concave shapes. Many ship's boats have concave curves at the stern where the side of the boat sweeps down to the keel in the transom area. If the moulding cannot reproduce this it can be simulated afterwards by either Isopon or Milliput. Figure 4 shows how. You will note that the moulded shape simply ignores the concave hollow, which is built up afterwards.

Ship's boats with square transoms cannot be satisfactorily moulded using this technique, as the necessary sharpness of the aft corners cannot be achieved. It is best in this case to lengthen the punch and die and make the aft end rounded to facilitate the moulding process. Subsequently fit a separate transom into the shell, cutting off the redundant round end. Make sure that the moulding is drawn deep enough to encompass the sheer of the boat. It is all too easy to stop the moulding process too soon. I find it best to attach a generously-sized keel before attempting any further work on the moulding. This will allow the moulding to be held in a vice whilst fitting out, etc. Only cut the keel down to size at the end. If the plug itself is cut down to the correct sheer it can be used, fitted into the moulding, as a guide when cutting down the moulding to the correct sheer.

All the interiors of the boats – inwales, timbers, floorboards, gratings, thwarts, etc. were made as etchings. The coloured rubbing strake on the outside was made from Letraset tape simply applied after the painting was finished. Two tips are important when using this method. Firstly do not stretch it when applying, as its adhesive will allow 'pull back' to take out the stretch thus leaving a gap at the end. Secondly, apply the slightest touch of cyano to the ends to stop the tape coming off later. Even the oars can be etched, although wire flattened at the blade end can also be used. Remember unless the boat is acting as a sea boat (*ie* swung out on the deck edge

Figure 4
Drawing showing aft section of a typical ship's boat and the use of filler to produce the concave shape between hull and keel

Required shape

Moulded shape

Moulded
shape

Glue

Added keel

Filler

Finished shape

on davits) the rudder should be unshipped and laid in the stern sheets. This was to prevent it swinging about.

Armament
The main armament of *Glorious* was sixteen 4.7in HA/LA Mk VIII on Mk XII mountings. These weapons had no shields so all the detail had to be included. These particular weapons were not widely used so information on them was scarce. According to Campbell in *Naval Weapons of WW2* these weapons were only mounted in *Nelson*, *Rodney*, *Courageous*, *Glorious*, *Albatross* and *Adventure*. I eventually obtained drawings from the gun manual, through the services of the Hampshire County Museum Service. Some of the parts

4.7in gun (finished gun on left, x2 mock-up in centre, brass and paper mock-up on right).

were made as lathe turnings but most of the parts were etched. The etching drawings were drawn twice-full size (as is the custom when drawing on a drawing board unlike computer-derived drawings which are drawn to size due to their greater accuracy) and, as a check, a twice-full size mock-up using the drawings was made up. The photograph on p.45 shows the x2 mock-up, a finished gun on the left hand side and a 1:1 paper mock-up.

The other main weapons were three 8-barrelled pom-poms, made largely from etchings with the barrels made from hypodermic needles, and two multi-barrelled 0.5in machine guns sited one forward on the starboard side and one aft on the port side. By the Second World War the latter were obsolete being largely ineffective against contemporary aircraft. The pom-pom was a better weapon but would have benefited from a greater range. However, the weapon had been developed in the 1920s when its design was seen as adequate.

Etched components

The use of photo etching has been discussed previously and was used extensively throughout the model. In certain areas its use was paramount in producing fine intricate detailing. The area under the extended round down was entirely made of etchings. All the supports and gangways were designed as etchings.

One problem was the safety nets on the catwalks. These were made, for the model, of the finest filter mesh and looked awful. On looking at pictures of the real vessel it was apparent that at any distance these nets of fine rope were not to be seen anyway so they were left off the model. A clear case of leaving out that which, if included, is going to be out of scale ie too large and obtrusive!

Etchings were also used on all four cranes. The ones under the round-down were interesting in that a fair bit of ingenuity was required to get the etching design to produce the shape of the crane.

The forward cranes when stowed were hinged half way along the jib to enable them to fit tidily against the hull.

The most delicate use of etchings was the wireless aerials spaced along the flight deck edge. Firstly, the design was not easy to determine, the position of the diagonals being complicated and it required much effort to unravel from the photos. Secondly, folding them up around a thin tapered Perspex former was a nightmare of the 'taking the tablets and lying in a darkened room' calibre. The result, however, was well worth the effort.

Aircraft

To model a carrier without her complement of aircraft would be like modelling a battleship without her guns. The information, including plans, was obtained from the book *British Naval Aircraft since 1912* by Owen Thetford and from companion books in the same series detailing the aircraft of individual manufacturers, *ie* Fairey, Blackburn, Hawker, etc. Correct-sized drawings were obtained by calculating the percentage difference between the correct scale wingspan and the size of the drawings shown in the book, and setting this percentage on a photocopier. If you do this check the result for accuracy before doing anything else. Always remember the old craftsman's saying: 'measure twice, cut once'. In case this is difficult to grasp here is an example:

Say the actual wingspan of the aircraft is 31ft 6in
At a scale of 1:192 this will be
$$\frac{31.5 \times 12 \times 25.4}{192} = 50\text{mm on the model}$$
(the 12 and 25.4 convert the answer to millimetres)
If the wingspan of the drawing in the book is 65mm
the percentage will be
$$\frac{50}{65} \times 100 = 76.9 \text{ per cent, say 77 per cent}$$

William Mowll's completed 1:48 scale working model of HMS *Warrior* at sea in August 1996. RAY BRIGDEN

(Left)
Detail of a GRP model hull surface showing deliberately rough texture of imitation iron plates, rivet lines, and rigols above the scuttles, all included in the moulding. These details are only visible when the light catches the hull surface, or when reflected in water.

(Below)
An external mix airbrush being used for general varnishing of the decks of the *Warrior* model.

(Top right)
Eric Dyke's HMS *Ocean*, 1900. Note the beautiful black, white and buff Victorian livery.

(Bottom right)
The funnels, boat deck, superstructure and masts of HMS *Ocean*.

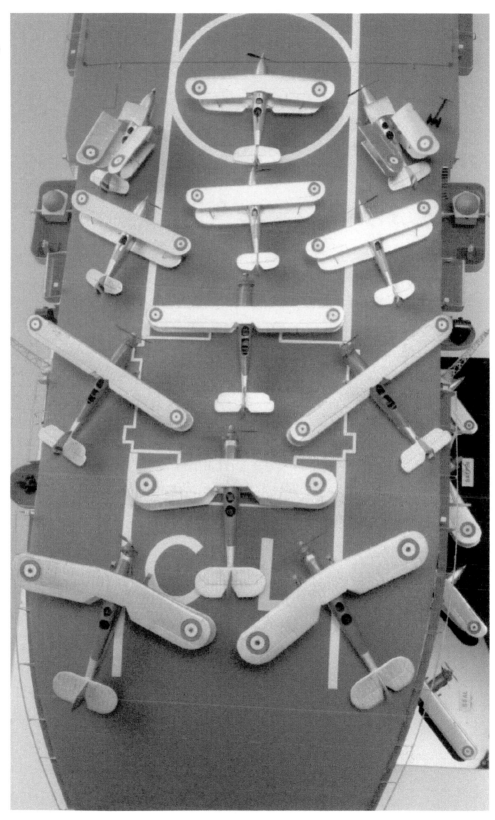

(Top left)
Detail of Brian King's model of the aircraft carrier HMS *Glorious*, looking up under the carrier round-down aft showing girder support, gangways and crane. Note also the night lifebuoy just to the right of the 4.7in gun.

(Bottom left)
Finished model of one of HMS *Glorious*'s Fairey Seal spotter-bombers to 1:192 scale. The actual wingspan of the model is 72mm.

(Right)
A aircraft strike on HMS *Glorious*'s flight deck, from above. Note aircraft with folded wings.

(Left)
Forward superstructure of Peter Beisheim's HMS *Hood* in 1:200 scale.
MORTEN SKOV

(Right)
Quarterdeck and X and Y turrets of HMS *Hood*. Note the 'trompe d'oeil' planked deck and the remains of the aircraft platform on the left side of X turret.
MORTEN SKOV

(Below)
C turret of Peter Beisheim's model of the Italian battleship *Vittorio Veneto*. Note the bare steel upper decks typical of Italian warships – only the quarterdeck is teak-planked.
KIM KANSTRUP

(Above)
Philip Baggaley's 1:1250 scale model of the Italian battleship *Roma*. Note how the aircraft on the after catapult add a touch of colour. The red and white aircraft recognition stripes on the forecastle and quarterdeck are authentic.

(Below)
Philip Baggaley's French battleship *Richelieu* showing her attractive second camouflage pattern. Her complex superstructure and multitude of light AA guns resulted in her taking over 1000 hours to build, incorporating over 1600 parts.

(Below)
Two versions of the popular Tamiya 1:350 scale *Fletcher* class destroyer kit built by Loren Perry, one *(above)* showing the *Charles Ausburn*e in 1942, the other showing her in 1944 with dazzle camouflage.

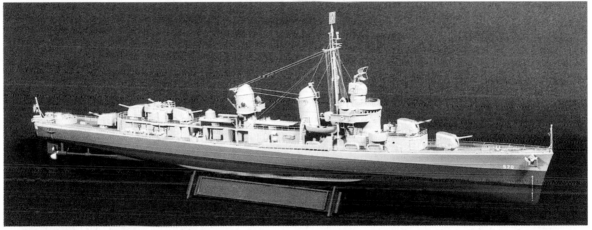

(Above)
Close-up of the bridge of Loren Perry's 1:429 scale Revell USS *Arizona*. A relief-etched range clock is seen just above the ship's bell. Reflective dummy headlight lenses for model railway locomotives are fitted to the searchlights on the funnel.

(Right)
The bridge of David Jack's *SC 1055*. The captain (centre) is converted from a traffic policeman figure.

(Above)
The completed 1:24 scale model of *SC 1055*, built by David Jack.

(Left)
Depth charge racks at the stern of *SC 1055*.

(Right)
Stephen Henninger's model of the USS *Enterprise*, on show at the National Air and Space Museum, Washington DC, the island is shown as originally built – and as it appeared in 1975. The 'beehive', or inverted thimble, contributed to the most distinctive look of any aircraft carrier. The model purposefully retains the original look, much preferred by its builder.
MARK HENNINGER

Natural sunlight from the National Air & Space Museum skylight ceiling illuminates the bow of the *Enterprise* model. The photo shows the catwalk, deck-edge curbing, catapult bridle arrester ramps, hose reels, ship's bell, whip antennae, mooring blocks, hull-side scaffolding eyelets, and drainage pipes. Five aircraft types can be seen on deck (front row: F-14; middle row ((right to left)): TA-4, EA-6; back row: A-7).

MARK HENNINGER

(Above)
David Merriman's 1:96 model of the SNN USS *Skipjack*, running submerged. The boat is painted in its pre-commissioning colour scheme to maximise underwater visibility for the operator. If you can't see it, you can't drive it!

(Left)
The authentically 'weathered' propeller of the *Skipjack*.

(Above)
The completed, well weathered, *Skipjack*
model. Note the subtle streaking of off-black
running from the periscope/mast wells

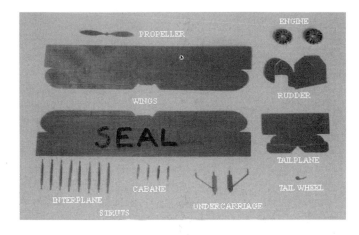

Set of etched parts
for a Seal aircraft
together with two
turned and machined
engine parts.

NB: you need to reduce the drawing size to 77 per cent not by 77%

Having set the date of 1936 for the model the aircraft on board would have been Baffins, Seals, Ospreys, and Nimrods, all canvas-covered biplanes. It was decided to build six of each, making a total of twenty-four planes to, some with folded wings. This was a big task and required all efforts to be directed to this job alone so work on the ship itself was put aside.

I decided to make the fuselages of wood and most of the rest as brass etchings or as turned parts. With models of this scale (1:192) the small components such as wing struts, propellers, under carriage struts, etc. lend themselves to etching and even the wings could be developed into flat blanks thus saving hours of work cutting them out. The photograph shows all the etched parts for a Seal aircraft and the two turned and milled parts for the engine.

Fuselages

These were made from cedar off cuts from a previously-made glass case. Cedar, in many ways, is ideal carving timber as it cuts well and is not too hard hence its use in pencil making. Aircraft fuselages are straightforward to carve but the problem lies in boring the holes for such things as under carriage components, cabane struts, tail skids, etc. This can be very difficult if it is attempted on a previously-carved hull as the drill simply slides about on the curved surface, not to mention the difficulty of establishing the correct position. A bit of lateral thinking was necessary to solve this problem. If the three-view drawing of the aircraft is examined the exact position of all the necessary holes is easily determined. Therefore why not drill the holes with the fuselage as a rectangular prism? No curved surfaces. The final shape of the fuselage can be carved afterwards.

If this is not clear, the fuselage was made as a rectangular prism of the correct overall size: same length, width and height as the finished job. A rectangular box jig was made to fit these fuselage blanks closely (see photograph below). On the flat surfaces of this jig all the holes were marked out and drilled with the appropriate sized drill as in the three-view drawing. The blanks were then simply loaded into the jig and drilled. All the holes were at right angles to the faces of course but the components could be bent to the correct angle after assembly. The blanks were then carved to shape. The wooden jig stood up to making six off – a much larger quantity would have required a metal jig.

Box jig for drilling
holes in an aircraft
fuselage (blank partly
inserted in jig) and
finished carved and
drilled fuselages.

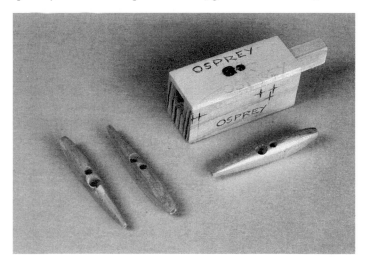

Aerofoil components

These comprise both sets of wings, tail plane and rudder. In every case they were etched as two surface blanks. See the photograph which shows at the top on the left-hand side - the assembly fixture for the lower wings; on the right – the assembly fixture for the upper wings; and below - the drawing template for the small etched parts. The top face in every case (or one side of the rudder) was etched to the correct shape whereas the lower adjoining surface was made larger than the correct shape. The two sections of each etching were lazily folded over so that the shaped top section lay over the other; the lazy fold becoming the leading edge. A piece of thin, shaped card or balsa was entrapped between the two pieces to form the aerofoil section before the open edges were soldered together with the lower surface cleaned up to match the already correctly-etched top shape.

With larger aircraft models, the ribs can be simulated by fairly heavily scribed lines on the inside surface of the blanks before folding up. This raises slight lines on the outside – the ribs. In the case of these smaller carrier aircraft the ribs were simulated by light pencil lines on the silver paint. The etchings also included the position of all the struts and the lines showing ailerons and elevators, which were

half etched in. Experience has shown it is easier to add these things at the drawing board stage rather than to wait and try to put them on the actual component.

The etched components such as struts needed to have extensions added to fit into their respective holes. The wing and cabane struts need really long extensions as it becomes very difficult to locate in some cases twelve struts into their respective wing holes. A case of three in and two out otherwise! The wing struts were fixed with cyano, which proved better than solder, before being cleaned up. Fixtures were made up to locate the sections: firstly to assemble the tail and lower wing(s) and secondly to locate the upper wing and these are shown in the photograph. Several aircraft were assembled with their wings folded. Tiny aircraft are difficult enough to make in their normal configuration - with their wings folded 'difficult' is not really the right word!

The aircraft at that time were all painted in silver dope apart from the roundels, squadron markings, letters and numbers. They were, therefore, sprayed with aluminium enamel paint kept well stirred. Many ways were tried to attach the roundels but eventually hand-drawn and painted ones were used. The size of these was a headache as every photo, even of the same type, showed a different size and position. It was about this time that the roundels were kept off control surfaces as it was found that the weight of paint tended to cause control surface flutter, exacerbated by the ground crews continually touching up the paintwork, particularly the blue, which cracked, flaked and faded quickly, adding undesired weight. For the same reason the red, white and blue stripes on the rudder were transferred to the fin. The composition

Aircraft assembly fixtures (lower and upper wings) and etching drawing template for the Seal.

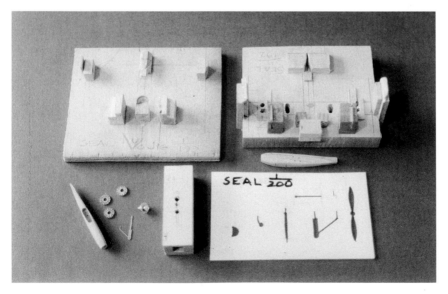

and relative position of the aircraft in the strike was decided in consultation with my friend, the late John Mackay, who had been a FAA pilot during the Second World War.

Finally, chocks were required both in front and behind the aircraft wheels in the strike on the flight deck. I filed a triangular prism on a length of brass rod and used this to make a series of triangular dents in a flattened piece of Plasticene. These were filled with a 'wipe' of Isopon. You can make thirty or forty in a few moments. Some will be no good as some of the indents do not fill properly but these can be discarded. When cleaned up no paint was required, as the natural grey colour seemed appropriate.

The end of *Glorious*

It perhaps remains to give an account of the very sad end to this fine ship that had given so much to the training of the FAA between the wars. The Norwegian campaign of 1940 was a disaster for the Allies with little real hope that our overstretched forces operating far from their bases could be victorious. Some battles were won but at the beginning of June 1940 it was decided to withdraw. *Glorious* set sail carrying RAF Hurricanes and Gladiators as well as her own aircraft. Their aircrews were also on board.

The only escort for the carrier, and we were very short of fast carriers at that time, was two destroyers, *Acasta* and *Ardent*. With no aircraft aloft they were intercepted by *Scharnhorst* and *Gneisenau* and all three ships were sunk with only forty-three survivors. *Acasta* managed to torpedo and damage *Scharnhorst* before being sunk herself. Why *Glorious* had no aircraft in the air is unbelievable but it was so. With proper air reconnaissance the tragedy might have been avoided. It was not and this loss followed the earlier sinking of her sister-ship *Courageous* on a fool's errand searching for U-boats in the Western approaches in September 1939. Five hundred and nineteen men lost their lives. All in all a very sad end for two fine ships. Having seen *Courageous* only four years previously I felt her loss keenly.

Aircraft strike on the flight deck from the port side (note aircraft with unfolded wings, Isopon chocks and black searchlight).

4

Scratch-Building Second World War Capital Ships in Plastic Card:
HMS *Hood* 1941

BY PETER BEISHEIM

Since the late 1970s scratch-building in medium or large scale to recreate the past has become my idea of warship modelling. The desire to see naval history in three dimensions, and the historical research behind the models, was further enhanced in 1978 when I went to the Public Record Office in London on a scholarship to complete my history thesis. I brought with me, apart from all my notes, what amounted to no less than a modeller's crisis: I had come to a stalemate in my conversion of 1:400 and 1:700 plastic kits,

a hobby which I had carried to a point where it had almost ceased to be a challenge. This kind of modelling was inextricably connected with my interest in naval history in general, and the history of the twentieth-century capital ship in particular. At that time a plastic kit in 1:400 scale took me about six months to convert into what I thought was a satisfactory model, and nevertheless friends and relations would see them as 'merely plastic kits'! So I suppose vanity was one of at least two driving forces behind my own

HMS *Hood* as in 1941. Note the simplified dry dock base.
KIM KANSTRUP

conversion to scratch-building. The other reason was the seemingly infinite number of odd scales marketed by plastic kit manufacturers (see Chapter 6). It was almost impossible to build up a collection of ships in one or two identical scales and, to make things even more frustrating, the renowned Japanese company Tamiya had just launched a new 1:350 scale series of models of Second World War battleships which looked extremely promising, but of course they did not fit in with my existing 1:400 models.

These factors combined made my decision for me, I felt that I had no other option but to turn to scratch-building. The next thing to do was to find an appropriate scale. This apparently minor problem took me quite a while to get settled, since there are numerous aspects to be considered if you expect to be able to build a collection.

Choice of Scale

This will almost inevitably depend on:
(A) Your facilities, *ie* the size of your home and workshop.
(B) Storage problems: Have you decided on a collection or just the 'once in a lifetime' model?
(C) Time factor: This comprises both the time at your disposal and the amount of time you want to spend on one model.

I soon came to realise that my 1:400 scale would be insufficient for the amount of detail I wanted to go with thorough historical research, so I decided to double it to 1:200 (metric equivalent of 1:192) which can be described as a medium to large scale, since a model of a Second World War battleship or carrier will have a length averaging 4ft (about 1.20m). It should be noted that the details in 1:200/1:192 are too delicate for R/C purposes.

Choice of Materials:

I have always found it extremely important to choose the right kind of material to suit both scale, type of model, your personal temper etc. In discussions with fellow modellers I have noticed that this is sometimes a controversial subject and surrounded by much tradition, habit, and even some prejudice. Wood still ranks high with many modellers, and I had tried to use various softwoods, but I discarded this for a number of reasons which derive mainly from my long experience in converting plastic kit models, having gained a lot of experience working with plastic card, or sheet styrene, as some prefer to call it. This has proved itself a very efficient material to obtain maximum definition and finish. Theoretically at least it requires hardly any surface treatment at all apart from the usual coat of paint – well, at least in theory, since all the joints and cementing and fillings need sanding just like any other material. I dare to claim that for superstructure hardly any other medium compares with plastic card, irrespective of scale, although for the hull this argument can be challenged, as it does not give the modeller the option of either solid hull or the 'bread and butter/sandwich' method, but leaves only the plank-on-frame option. Consequently styrene hulls have their optimal range in small or medium scale, *ie* up to 1:192; larger than that they tend to be extremely hard to handle and a veritable nightmare to sand. Another important reason for deciding to carry on in plastic as a scratch-modeller was the 'desk-top' modelling mentality one is privileged to develop over the years as a plastic kit converter. Having spent years in a cosy corner of the living room listening to, more than watching, television does not make the garage or a cold and poorly-lit basement room a particularly attractive modelling environment. The hull building procedure is likely to be set in such surroundings, however, unless you can plan to start your new model in late spring or early summer entertaining your next-door neighbour with your (less than) noiseless tools.

Choice of Subject

Another important item to be considered when starting your career as a warship modeller is your preferred type and exact period of warship. Looking at articles and books on warship models proves that this is subject to personal preference and bias, not to mention aesthetics. The rare combination of beauty and awe in a capital ship from the two World Wars has been a source of inspiration to many modellers and made my choice an easy one, although I must confess that the cruiser of the same period is certainly no less attractive. Anyone who has been interested in naval history and the Second World War must have been impressed by the beautiful lines of HMS *Hood*, and many modellers have tried, with more or less success, to recreate them. This has led to the assertion that famous ships like the *Hood* and *Bismarck* are hackneyed subjects and should be discarded by the serious modeller. I cannot disagree more after the pleasure and challenge of researching and building her. The real problem is that the modeller tends to become too absorbed with details and either gradually, as I have already said, becomes unable to complete the model, or overloads it with details disproportionate to the scale. To find an acceptable compromise is a necessity to the modeller.

Waterline versus Full-Hull Models

The first time I visited the Imperial War Museum in London I was very impressed by the Norman Ough waterline models exhibited there, and they became my major source of inspiration for a number of years. Consequently I started out building waterline models with the modest ambition to outdo the details and finish of the best plastic kit then available. However, as my experience increased, so did my demands for details and quality until it became hard even to complete a model with the amount of detail I wanted to show. While I was building waterline models, I had also for some time been studying a 1972 article in *Warship International* which showed some very clear 1918 photographs of the *Hood* on the building slip. These gave me an idea of the correct shape of the conspicuous keel plating and the positions of at least some of the sea valves. They also gave me the appearance of the friction damage protection which ran like long narrow rails on the upper part of her torpedo bulge. I became so inspired that I decided to have a go at a full-hull model. Until then I had always been a bit sceptical about them, since the typical so-called full-hull model would show only details from the waterline upwards and hardly any underwater details and could most properly be termed 'waterline models with simplified keels'.

So it was not just a question of building the full hull including as much detail below the waterline as could possibly be researched, there remained also the question of where and upon what to place the finished product. This came fairly easy: I had for some time been looking at models of major warships in recent books and

Port side view of the model. Overall photographs of long models such as this are rarely satisfactory.
KIM KANSTRUP

magazines displayed on a stylised or simplified dry dock base with decent results. Of course, a simplified dry dock cannot pretend to be like Norman Ough's 'Dorsetshire in Dry Dock' diorama which used to be exhibited at the Imperial War Museum. This kind of base represents a compromise in realism and exposed underwater details. I leave it to the reader to apply his own judgement. I have since then been 'hooked' on full hull models. It did, however, almost turn against me when I decided to make a model of the German battleship *Bismarck* after the *Hood* was completed in the mid-1990s. What I seem to have forgotten after years of modelling mainly British warships was that German ships were about 90 per cent welded and do not show the characteristic overlappings on the hull so attractive to the modeller and a distinct feature of the keel.

Plans and Historical References

To acquire realistic plans – particularly correct and detailed ones – is a constant source of concern to the serious warship modeller. I think that most experienced modellers will agree that the epithet 'historically correct plans' is little more than pretentious advertising, and once purchased, particularly via mail-order, they often turn out to be a disappointment. Let there be no doubt that all plans, whatever claims may be made for them, need to be thoroughly researched before being trusted. Another question that needs to be considered is the fact that most major warships have a lifespan of at least twenty years and may look very different at the end of their careers than they did during their first period of commission. The *Hood* proved no exception to this rule: in spite of the popular misunderstanding that her appearance changed little throughout the 1920s and 1930s and first two years of the war, this was not so, although it has some justification regarding her obsolescent armour scheme which may have contributed to her loss when she fell victim

to the Bismarck's 15in guns sixty years ago. (I refer the reader to W J Jurens' article 'The loss of HMS *Hood* – a Re-examination', and the book *The Bismarck Chase* by Robert J Winklareth.)

In general most plans offer little or no underwater detail. Consequently many other photographic sources had to be consulted to supplement my plans before I was able to move on to this. As I had chosen to make my model of the ship as she appeared in her final shape in May 1941, it was necessary to locate exactly how much her waterline/boot-topping had moved upwards and decreased her freeboard over the inter-war period as her displacement had increased considerably above that originally planned. So I realised once again that good plans from renowned firms and artists are not sufficient: the modeller has to do his own historical research during the building process. This process is subsequently much prolonged and the modeller often frustrated when he has to go back and change what has already been constructed and attached to the model. This also serves to make modelling a more intellectualised process and may prove distasteful to the traditional modeller who is mainly focused on the craftsman's side of warship modelling. Luckily an almost infinite amount of reference material on Second World War warships is available today in book form and can easily be obtained and reduced/magnified in scale on your home computer.

Researching HMS Hood 1941

I had already bought a set of Norman Ough plans for the model from Maritime Models in Greenwich some years before launching the project. These plans, like others I have seen, represent the ship as she appeared in her 'classical shape' during the 1930s, so they had to be supplemented by other plans to be able to make the model as in 1941. John Roberts' plans and drawings in *Anatomy of the Ship: The Battle Cruiser Hood* have served as some of my main sources. Since then similar plans and drawings have been published in a number of books and magazines. For anyone who can read Polish (and also for those like me who cannot) the monograph *Monografie Morskie No 6* is recommended for its plans and drawings of the ship in her final configuration. I obtained my copy via the White Ensign Models home pages.

Having studied the *Hood* over a number of years one tends to develop the idea that the amount of photographs published is almost unlimited. Indeed the photographic material representing the ship from her first commission in 1920 until the outbreak of war in 1939 is very large. However, after September 1939, and particularly after her last refit in January-March 1941, this dries up and almost disappears. The last photos of the ship grant the modeller very few details, and some of the final changes seem to be more or less guesswork. My favourite publications from the 1970s are *Warship Profile No. 19* HMS *Hood Battle Cruiser 1916–1941*, and *Ensign Special/Man of War: Hood: Design and Construction*. I have already mentioned the article by W J Jurens for studies of hull details. Alan Raven and John Roberts' book *British Battleships of World War II* from 1976 is excellent for both photos and plans and information. Other books and publications have since been published, I need only mention *British Battleships 1919–1939* by R A Burt, Arms & Armour Press 1993, and the recently published *Monografie Morskie No 6: Hood*. For the users of the Internet I can warmly recommend a close study of The HMS *Hood* Association Website, it is inexhaustible as source material and never dries up as it is currently updated as new information constantly appears. For the major alterations after the outbreak of the war please see the photographs and their captions.

Building the Hull (simplified account)

When it was decided to write this book, to give it a sort of uniqueness, it was agreed among the contributors that each chapter should be given a special topic of its own.

This was done to give the entire book a consistency in subject-matter and to avoid the individual chapters appearing as no more than a series of unconnected articles. Besides the general principles of historical modelling the emphasis of this chapter is on Second World War battleship armament and the modelling of it, and on deck construction methods on models of major warships. Consequently other items like the hull and basic superstructure will be dealt with only cursorily.

I began the difficult and laborious process of transferring the plans from paper to styrene sheets after having them re-scaled from 1:192 to metric 1:200. When I was drawing the first thing I realised was that the contour lines of the frames of my plans were of limited value if I wanted to take full advantage of the armour belt possibilities in the styrene sheets. The armour belts on the *Hood* were of markedly different thickness and could be much more accurately imitated if added independently after the hull had been sanded - somewhat reminiscent of the procedure in building the real ship. The beginner (and I was once one myself) must remember that the measurements of the frames once transferred from plans to plastic card must be reduced exactly as the thickness of the planks later to be added as 10mm plastic strips, 1.5mm thick. Once this in my opinion somewhat tedious process was completed and the filling out and sanding had been accomplished, I had the pleasure of being able to proceed to the more 'historical' part of the hull: the armour belts and other hull details. HMS *Hood* had three main armour belts attached to her sides: an upper belt of 5in, a middle belt of 7in, and a waterline main belt of 12in. It turned out that these were in fact rather easy to imitate with different gauges of Evergreen plastic card which came almost precise to scale thickness.

Nothing looks more uninteresting than a model with no hull detail or plating created by riveting overlappings. Unfortunately this argument will relegate major German and American warships of the Second World War to the modeller's second choice since these were predominantly welded and showed no visible plating on the hull. To transfer the plating of a major warship on to a model is a time-consuming but also challenging process since it necessitates some experimentation. I first tried to apply the thinnest gauge Evergreen sheets which came fairly close to scale, but even these became too conspicuous to appear convincing on the model and, furthermore, tended to crease up, not being able to withstand the plastic cement. So I had to do some experimenting with two or three extra coats of paint carefully masked off with sticky tape. These left a very fine edge which even then required some cautious sanding with very fine sandpaper. The sea valves were easy enough to manufacture by cutting plastic tube of a suitable gauge into very short pieces and fitting them into pre-drilled holes in the keel after which the edges were sanded down. What turned out to be the main problem was to find exactly where to put them in spite of the amount of photographic evidence available.

Decks

The forecastle deck and quarter deck on a major British warship of that period are her upper decks ie visible to the viewer. These decks were covered by a layer of teak planks which is one of the first things an experienced modeller tends to look at when appraising a ship model. There are two to three distinguishable methods of imitating a bleached teak deck on a battleship or a cruiser: (A) to manufacture and lay the planks individually as preferred in larger scales;

(B) to paint the deck in a basic colour and draw the caulking lines by a ruler and either Indian ink or pencil; or (C) to paint the majority of the planks individually according to the 'trompe-l'oeil' principle known from art. As for method (A) I need not remind the reader that just because a planked wooden deck may look beautiful on a model - and follows to some extent how a real deck is planked - it does not necessarily follow that it will look realistic on the scaled-down model. In the end I gave it up in favour of method (C) which, although it is nearly as time-consuming as method A, has since then become my approach and will be explained in detail.

Trompe-l'oeil Planked Decks

I started out by painting the entire deck a 'dry beach' colour to approximate the general hue of bleached teak. This I allowed to dry up, after which I applied two slightly different versions of the same colour in large irregular spots, one lighter and paler and one darker and warmer. The deck now appeared rather distressingly like a leopard skin and had to be sanded with fine grained paper to remove any edges and sharp changes. After sanding came the difficult and laborious procedure of drawing the individual planks/caulking by ruler and

Top view of A and B turrets and the *'trompe d'oeil* planked deck.
KIM KANS I HUP

(right)
Y turret and quarterdeck. Note the simulated planking.
KIM KANSTRUP

(below)
C turret of the Italian battleship *Vittorio Veneto*. Note the bare steel upper decks typical of Italian warships - only the quarterdeck is teak-planked.
KIM KANSTRUP

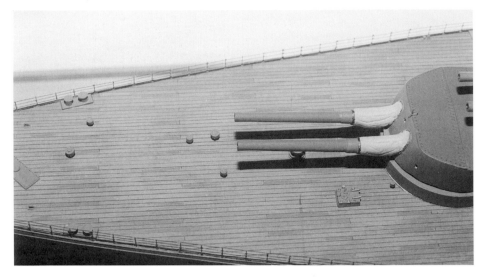

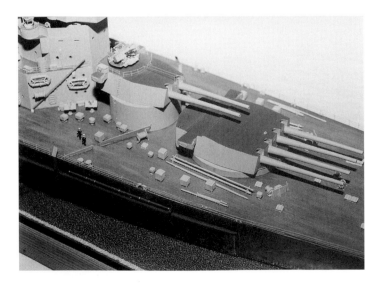

with a very thin pencil, which needed constant sharpening during the process. It is extremely important to find the distance between the lines according to the scale or the final result will look unrealistic. Having seen some 'pyjamas'-like results produced by Indian ink I have come to prefer pencil lines to imitate caulking. They hold the advantage that they are dark grey and not jet black, bearing in mind that the colours of a model must always follow the scale reduction. (The general principles for painting warship models will be explained later). After the planks had been drawn I proceeded to paint about one-third to half the boards to recreate the realistic variation, particularly at the joints. When this had been allowed to dry up completely, I gave the entire deck a coat of matt finish to remove the slight gloss from the pencil lines and to protect the deck against undesirable fingerprints. This proved essential since a lot of handling of the hull remained for the rest of the building process. For an assessment of the final result, see the photograph in the

(left)
A and B turrets of HMS *Duke of York* as in 1943. Note the camouflaged main deck. The dark/medium grey paint is wearing through and the natural colour of the teak planks is faintly visible.
KIM KANSTRUP

colour section. Also, compare the decks of the Hood to the decks of the Italian battleship *Vittorio Veneto* of 1941. Note that according to Italian capital ship and cruiser construction custom there was no layer of teak on the main deck, only their quarter decks had this arrangement. Also compare the Hood's clean decks with the heavily camouflaged main deck of the King George V class battleship hms Duke of York as in 1943 (opposite). It is virtually impossible to see the planking in spite of the fact that the dark grey camouflage paint has become somewhat transparent by wear and tear from both crew and weather. Camouflage on teak decks became common later during the war. Both models are waterline 1:200 scale which I completed in 1986 and 1988 respectively.

Armament

The *Hood* carried eight 15in guns in four Mk 2 twin turrets as her main armament. This turret arrangement seemed to have become the classical main armament for British battleships and battlecruisers in the final years of the First World War. However, the shape of the *Hood's* Mk2. turrets differed somewhat from those of the *Queen Elizabeth* and the *Royal Sovereign* class battleships and the battlecruisers *Renown* and *Repulse*. They were more

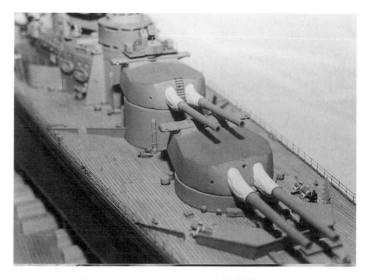

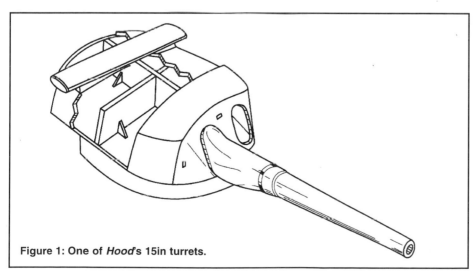

Figure 1: One of *Hood's* 15in turrets.

(top)
The two forward turrets of HMS *Hood*. Although this layout of the main armament produced a longer and heavier ship, it was probably the most reliable and versatile for ships of this period.
KIM KANSTRUP

(middle)
The impressive conning tower of the *Hood*. Note the UP launcher mounting on top of B turret, and the quadruple 0.5in machine-guns just aft of it on either side.
KIM KANSTRUP

(right)
The aft end of *Hood*'s
shelter deck showing
the 8-barrelled pom-
pom mounting offset
to starboard.
KIM KANSTRUP

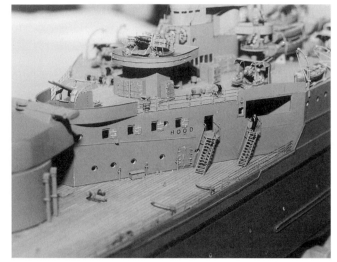

(below)
Another view of the
after superstructure.
Note the details
behind the open 4in
gun shield.
KIM KANSTRUP

spacious and had 30ft
rangefinders with sighting
hoods to replace the 15ft
rangefinders of the
previous designs. The
main difference was
to be found in their
interior construction:
improved flash-tightness
made the *Hood* the only
'Post-Jutland' ship for
some years after the
war, incorporating
lessons learned from the
disastrous experiences of
the Battle of Jutland.
This also meant that the *Hood* was given
low priority for substantial reconstruction,
the surviving earlier units of the *Queen
Elizabeth* class and the *Renown* being
rebuilt first, and the outbreak of war meant
she was never modernised. The main
turrets were manufactured from medium
(1mm) gauge plastic card supported by
frames. I prefer a hollow structure to a
solid one, as I think it gives a better finish
and true-to-scale measurements and is far
superior when it comes to cutting sighting
ports. I have tried to illustrate by line
drawings the procedure of the main
armament turret (Figure 1). The 15in gun
barrels were moulded according to a
turned master. The photographs show her

(right)
The forward turrets of
Vittorio Veneto.
Despite its relative
complexity and size
the triple turret
became almost the
standard main
armament mounting
for Second World
War battleships.
KIM KANSTRUP

A and B turrets, and her impressive conning tower and the rear part of B turret and the UP launcher platform. Note the remains of the aircraft platform on X turret. The *Hood* carried observation planes for a short period in the 1920s on B and X turrets. This is the reason that the 8-barrelled pom-pom mount is placed slightly to starboard of the centreline since an aircraft crane was placed in this area and later removed (see photograph). For the characteristic boltheads found on capital ship turret tops I used a darning needle to press dents into the turret roofs. These dents were subsequently filled up with paint which formed a clearly defined bubble and was allowed to dry up. Then I used a sharp, soft pencil to make a very slight dark grey dent in the top of the bubbles. I believe the result gives a good illusion in this scale. Compare the *Hood*'s twin turrets with the typical Second World War triple turrets on the *Vittorio Veneto*, and the quadruple turrets of *Duke of York*.

As an historian and a modeller I have followed but not participated in the controversy over battleship armour schemes, main armament, and dual-purpose secondary armament etc, in books and publications over the last couple of decades. A similar discussion seems to be raging on several popular battleship websites on the Internet. I think it would be beyond the scope of this book to go into that. The advantages and disadvantages of twin turrets and triple turrets can be debated for ever, as can dual-purpose armament, and contracted versus divided armour schemes on these ships. The parameters are simply too many. But the reader should be warned of assumed objectivity supported by figures to cover chauvinism, and revisionist tendencies presently in vogue to degrade, against any cost in credibility, the design of German ships in particular.

Secondary armament

The original secondary armament of HMS *Hood* consisted of twelve 5.5in guns in single mounts. As they were removed in 1940 (before the configuration of my version), I shall limit myself to the gun mounts visible on the model, the sixteen 4in dual-purpose guns in twin mounts she carried from 1940 till the end of her career in May 1941. The shields of these mounts were open to the rear, one of the favourite arrangements of a detail-focused modeller like myself. It can be a great temptation to lose oneself in details since plans and

The 4in DP secondary armament of *Hood*. Compare this with the more modern twin 5.25in DP mounting on *Duke of York*.
KIM KANSTRUP

A good view of an open 4in shield.
KIM KANSTRUP

drawings of these are almost always in a much bigger scale; I think the true master is he who can limit himself to a suitable compromise between scale and the amount of detail on the real thing. It took me quite some time to identify and draw the basis for this complicated mount. Once this had been achieved I started the task of building

the mount step by step. To be able to use a styrene sheet close enough to scale thickness these had to be supported by very small frames. The barrels were handmade from Evergreen tube. This is a very tricky process since they have to absolutely identical, not only to the naked eye, but also to a fellow modeller with a magnifying

The twin 5.25in DP secondary armament of *Duke of York*. Note also the pom-poms (above) and 20mm Oerlikons (above right).
KIM KANSTRUP

The 90mm stabilised AA mounts on *Vittorio Veneto*. The 6in secondary armament turret can also just been seen in the lower right-hand corner. Only the US Navy and the Royal Navy used genuinely dual-purpose secondary armament in this period.
KIM KANSTRUP

glass. Compare this relatively light secondary armament arrangement with the modern dual-purpose arrangement on *Duke of York* as in 1943. The 5.25in twin mounting of the *King George V* class was the first (and last) solid structure I have made as a scratch builder, and I am far from satisfied with the result. The Italians chose a rather different solution for the *Vittorio Veneto*: six single stabilised 90mm AA guns on each side – perhaps too far ahead of their time to be successful. Also note the 6in secondary armament in triple turrets.

Eight-barrelled 2pdr pom-poms
The eight-barrelled 2pdr anti-aircraft armament on Second World War British battleships remain my personal favourite as a modeller. This mounting must be the most complex piece of equipment likely to be found on any warship. They were, like their German twin-barrel 37mm hand-loaded counterpart, not very successful, and were later replaced in the Royal Navy by the highly successful American quadruple 40mm Bofors mountings. Most plans and drawings of these sadly neglect to show the construction of the open mount 'step-by-step', and the research sometimes

Figure 2: Assembly of a pom-pom.

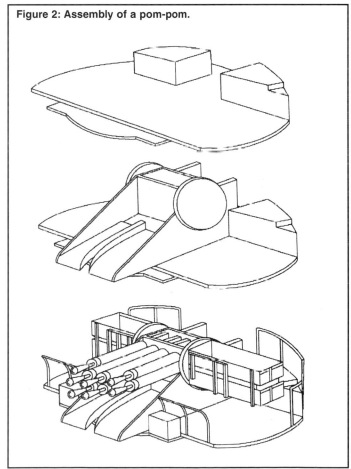

takes longer than the actual building process. I have tried to show 'exploded views' or the step-by-step procedure in line drawing (Figure 2). I should point out that the purpose of three-dimensional drawings is not to impress the viewer by draftsmanship nor to show as many details as possible – quite the opposite! Their purpose is to illustrate in a simplified way what detailed plans normally do not give the modeller, *ie* how to get started and then later to add details. Apart from the usual sheet styrene, stretched plastic sprue played a major part in the manufacturing of details. Luckily the funnel-shaped muzzle brakes gave me a good opportunity to use my miniature dentist's drills to add a touch of realism by drilling out the eight barrels of each mounting

UP mountings

Several British capital ships carried the highly innovative Unrotated Projectile (UP Mountings) in 1940-1. This weapon fired a 3in rocket containing an aerial mine to a height of 1000ft where it exploded to release a parachute which let down the mine on a wire. The intention was to let a veritable cloud of these hang in the air and hope that low-flying torpedo planes would hit the wire and explode the mine. Each mounting carried twenty smoothbore barrels. The weapon system proved unsuccessful since the mine-carrying parachutes tended to drift back onto the ships that had fired them. The ready-use lockers for the projectiles also proved a hazard to the *Hood*, catching fire in the early stages of the battle in the Denmark Strait (but not causing the final explosion). The mountings on other battleships were subsequently replaced by 8-barrel pom-poms. The box-like appearance of the UP mountings did not offer the modeller much challenge compared to the complexity of the pom-poms.

As close defence against low flying aircraft the *Hood* also carried four quadruple 0.5in machine gun quadruple mountings. The starboard side torpedo hatches are visible just below the degaussing coil.

A good view of one of *Hood*'s 8-barrelled pom-poms and the unsuccessful UP rocket launcher.
KIM KANSTRUP

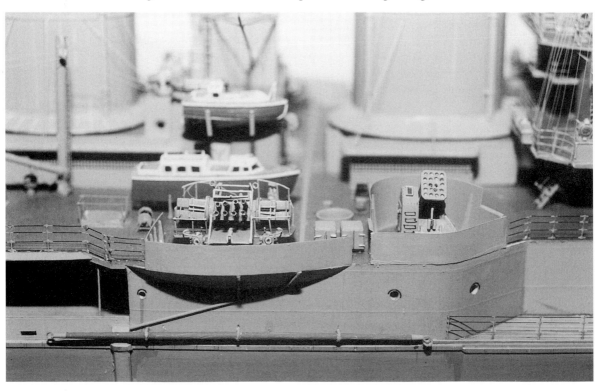

Painting Second World War Warship Models: How to Add a Touch of Realism to Warship Modelling.

As a frequent visitor to maritime museums in Europe and America I have often been impressed by the size and complexity of their warship models, but not by the unrealistically pristine finish of their paintwork. I should like to give a few suggestions on how to 'add a touch of realism to historical warship modelling'. Glossy paint on models tends to give the impression of a well-polished new car more than the weathered and often damaged colours of a warship in active service. I would like to refer the reader to Larry Sowinski's book *US Navy Camouflage of World War Two Era* (Floating Dry Dock 1976) which contains a good presentation of the matt finish of warships. I also highly recommend Alan Raven's recently published *Warship Perspectives: Camouflage*, Vol. 1 – 2, Royal Navy 1939-1941 and 1942, and David Williams, *Naval Camouflage 1914-1945*. The basic rule the serious warship modeller must observe is that the colours of any model must follow the scale! Consequently anything white on the real ship must countered by a very light grey on, for example, a 1:192 model, black (like boot-topping or funnel caps) must come out as very dark grey on the model etc. A dull brick red mixed with a bit of light grey for the keel looks far more realistic than the bright red that often ruins the overall impression of a good model. Camouflage on warships gives the modeller a good chance to deviate from the usual variations of grey and is fun to research. Unfortunately camouflage is sometimes scorned by certain model organisations, and some modellers, since it has a tendency to hide details and even a flawed finish, as it is sometimes claimed. I do not agree with this tendency, and the colours of a ship model should always be in accordance with the period and configuration that it is supposed to represent. I also think it works wonders of realism to add a bit of patina/weathering to your model. Rust, or dirty shades of a previous camouflage scheme which peeks through the present coat of paint, may give the finished model just what it needs to be a convincing miniature replica of the real ship at a given period of time. At the time of her loss the *Hood* was painted in an overall scheme of 507B, the medium grey variant of the British warship standard grey. In spite of the relatively short duration of her last commission it was already weathered by the heavy seas of the North Atlantic when she met her fate in May 1941.

5
Miniature Warships of the Second World War

BY PHILIP BAGGALEY

I used to make model warships to 1:600 scale but my modelling changed when in 1974, I bought the English language edition of Siegfried Breyer's monumental book *Battleships and Battle Cruisers 1905-1970*. It contained over 900 drawings of capital ships to a scale of 1:1250 and I thought it would be a challenge to make models to that scale. At that stage I assumed that the drawings would be sufficient by themselves, not realising that I would also need larger scale drawings and also photographs to make a satisfactory model. However, all credit to Herr Breyer for giving me the inspiration.

This scale, 1:1250, is rather on the small side for a miniature. Other miniature scales are 1:300, 1:384, 1:600, 1:700 and 1:1200, but most of my comments below apply whatever scale is chosen.

Choice and date of model

Theoretically the choice of the warship to be modelled is nearly limitless, but there are various practical considerations. Firstly, a novice modeller should not choose a complicated vessel. If the modeller has not built a battleship before it should be one with a relatively simple superstructure, such as a *Nelson* or *Bismarck* class, rather than one with a complicated superstructure such as the *Richelieu* or most Japanese battleships. Secondly, do not start a model unless one has adequate plans and preferably photographs. The best position to be in is to have more information than you think that you will need to complete the model and you will probably find that it will all be useful in the end.

The date at which the vessel is to modelled should be decided before

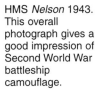

HMS *Nelson* 1943. This overall photograph gives a good impression of Second World War battleship camouflage.

construction starts. Firstly, warships are usually altered substantially in the course of their lives. In the case of a battleship it may have been reconstructed once or twice, and between reconstructions it may have had several minor refits. As the Second World War progressed, warships often had aircraft, catapults and boats removed and radar aerials and liferafts added and the light anti-aircraft (AA) armament greatly augmented. Secondly, the camouflage scheme often varied considerably over a ship's service life. As a very rough guide at the beginning of the war warships were usually painted in one colour, normally dark grey. As the war progressed multicolour camouflage schemes were introduced, British ones generally having curved or irregular patches of colour, whereas German and Italian ones had straight line or 'splinter' demarcation, and the United States Navy used various numbered 'Measures' for camouflage, some of which were curved and others were straight-line schemes. Towards the end of the war, because extensive use of radar made them nearly superfluous, camouflage schemes often became simpler again. Difficulty in obtaining details of a camouflage scheme may prevent a modeller from making a model at a particular date.

Paints

I use Humbrol paints because of their ready availability, but other manufacturers are Revell, Tamiya and Testor. Although a considerable number of colours may have been intended for a specific model aircraft or railway use, if these are the colour and shade that you need, use them.

I have had various problems with paints. These comments relate to my experience with Humbrol paints, but I suspect that similar problems may arise with paints from other manufacturers. The worst problem is that matt colours sometimes have a slight gloss, despite adequate stirring. My solution if a new tin of paint is slightly glossy is to stir it thoroughly and then to remove approximately the top one-tenth of the paint with a paint brush and throw the paint away. This usually solves the problem. Matt black is often the most troublesome colour.

Another problem is that various tins of the same colour can differ slightly in shade. I have heard of a modeller who buys, say, six tins of a particular colour before starting a model and then mixes them all to ensure a uniform shade. Also, sometimes a paint which has been in use for a considerable time suddenly becomes

The German battleship *Tirpitz* - another good example of camouflage.

thick and lumpy. In that case it should be thrown away, as adding thinner will not solve the problem.

It is often difficult to find information about a particular camouflage colour scheme for a warship and any colours in a book should be treated with caution. For example, two periodicals by the same American publisher showed camouflage schemes with colour chips of 'haze gray', which were both stated to be the true colour. Unfortunately there was a considerable difference in shade between them. Sometimes if the information is conflicting all that a modeller can do is to make an inspired guess about which is more likely to be correct.

As far as brushes are concerned, always try to buy the most expensive sable brushes from a local art shop. For very fine work I use a No. 1 brush, rather than 0 or 00. The reason is that there are so few bristles on an 0 or 00 brush that it carries very little paint and this is likely to dry too quickly. Also I have recently started selecting brushes by the shape of the bristles, rather than just choosing by number, as this can vary considerably between brushes of the same number.

Some specialist firms produce colour chips of naval greys. The Floating Drydock (for address see in Sources) produces US Navy colour chips. USN, Royal Navy and Imperial Japanese navy colour ships are available from Snyder and Short Enterprises, PMB 224, 9175 Kiefer Boulevard, Sacramento, California 95826-5105, U.S.A. Interestingly the Japanese Navy greys differ slightly depending which shipyard built or refitted the vessel in question.

Equipment and Tools

Fortunately the equipment and tools needed are relatively few, compared to the lathes and power tools needed for large scale models. For me the two most important items of equipment are a fluorescent table light and an Optivisor. I use a fluorescent light, even in daylight, as it gives even illumination on the worktable and unlike an ordinary table light, produces no heat, which is important for close work. An Optivisor is American, but there are also similar British products on the market with different brand names. It looks rather like welder's goggles and in mine the lenses have a magnification of x2, although lenses of higher magnification are available. It is ideal for working on small parts, and as a bonus since you are seeing the item twice the normal size, the standard of workmanship automatically goes up.

The *Roma* - close-up of superstructure and secondary armament.

Tools are a matter of preference and obviously vary somewhat from modeller to modeller. The tools that I use are a hacksaw and a small craft saw, scalpels using blades 10A and 11, double-edged razor blades, fine needle files both flat sided and rounded, dividers, a small hand drill with a set of fine drills and various grades of fine sandpaper. For cutting paper, which I use extensively for the superstructure platforms, I use a scalpel and cut along the edge of a steel rule. I also use a calculator for reducing dimensions on larger scale plans.

I started modelling using imperial measures but I have now been converted to the simplicity of metric. For measuring I use steel rules of different lengths but the most important criterion is that the markings on the rule should be clear and easy to read. Dividers are also useful if you need to take a measurement off a model. I have a glass kitchen cutting board on my table, which I use for a working surface. Such a board is usually slightly uneven on the top and smooth underneath so I use it upside down as a smooth surface is essential for cutting.

Materials

I am a traditional modeller and my main material is lime wood which is straight-grained and hard but not too hard. Other modellers have great success in using plastic card for warship models, but I do not know how well this would work for such a small scale as 1:1250.

I also find that cocktail sticks are invaluable. I originally used these for the main armament of battleships but I now use them for the secondary armament as well, as pins normally do not have the correct taper. Using a needle file and fine sandpaper, a cocktail stick can be tapered down to thinner than a fine pin. Modellers should cultivate the habit of looking at simple household items to see if they could serve some totally different modelling use!

I use paper for the vertical sides of the superstructure platforms, and pins and wire of assorted thickness for light AA guns and mast fittings. An easy way to straighten wire is to roll it firmly between a steel rule and a glass cutting board.

Construction

Generally there are no right or wrong methods as long as the result is satisfactory. Although I use one method of construction another method may be equally as good. Also what suits one person may not suit another but what matters is the standard of the finished model.

Hull

One point has to be decided first. Most warships have sheer, ie a rise in the height of the hull towards the bows. The modeller must decide whether to carve the hull in one piece, or to use a separate piece of wood for the sheer. A single piece of wood avoids the problem of a joint showing where the sheer ceases, but it leaves the problem that once the sheer has been carved the remainder of the top deck of the hull has to be shaped accurately parallel to the waterline. I prefer to use two pieces of wood, even though this leaves a join between the sheer and the remainder of the hull. It is often possible to disguise the join if it is on the line of a breakwater or other deck equipment. I take a tracing of the hull at deck level, and then with a biro and carbon paper draw the outline on the wood selected for the hull. Once this has been shaped roughly, I repeat the process for the outline of the hull at the waterline. For my last model I tried a different method as I took numerous dimensions from a larger scale plan and using a calculator reduced these to 1:1250 scale. I then plotted the points on the wood and joined up the points and I found this more accurate than using a 1:1250 plan.

Once the hull has been roughly shaped I then shape the bows, which together with the funnel seem to be the most important parts of the model to get

(left)
USS *Alabama* 1945.

(middle)
Alabama - note the
two-tone colour
scheme typical of
late-war US
battleships.

(bottom)
Alabama - note the
compactness of this
class of battleship.

'right'. I once tried using a template for
shaping the hull but I did not find this very
successful due to the small scale. Almost all
warships have flare at the bows, *ie* the hull
is narrow at the waterline and wider at
deck level to enhance its seakeeping
qualities. I shape this by eye using the
'lines' on the set of plans or a close-up
photo of the bows if available. The flare is
almost always concave and the basic rule is
to remove the minimum amount of wood
each time, as excessive enthusiasm in
removal can ruin the hull in an instant.

Another problem with the hull is the
anti-torpedo 'bulge' if this extends above
the waterline, or alternatively, particularly
in battleships, the armoured belt, which
often protrudes from the hull in a
rectangular box. My method is to carve the
amidships section of the hull with the sides
vertical, then mark the bulge or armoured
belt and gradually work at the hull with
a double-edged razor blade and fine
sandpaper until the bulge or belt is left
protruding.

The next item to be tackled is the
portholes, or more correctly the scuttles. I
used to paint them but found it difficult to
get identical-sized circles. A Rotring pen
can be used for this, but I have not tried
this method. I drill a hole with a fine drill

and then paint the inside black. Whatever the method used, the most important part is to mark the position of the scuttles accurately. If you have both a 1:1250 plan and a larger-scale plan, it is best to check the former against the latter and correct the positions if necessary, as these are often not accurate on the smaller-scale plan. When the positions have been checked, I mark these on tracing paper, sellotape the paper onto the hull and prick through the paper with a fine pin to mark the positions. As it can be difficult to align a long strip of paper accurately, I cut the paper up into three or four pieces and then stick and prick out each section separately onto the hull.

A few warships have larger square windows, normally on the bridge, or on the quarterdeck of a battleship, if it has a sternwalk and admiral's cabin. In that case I use the very thin paper which is made for rolling cigarettes. A piece is painted black to the appropriate height of the windows and a long strip is then cut off using a scalpel and a steel rule. This strip is then cut vertically for the individual windows, which are glued into position. As cigarette paper is so thin any protrusion is hardly noticeable.

Superstructure

For a battleship it is very useful if plans can be obtained showing each deck level of the superstructure. A monolithic block superstructure such as the one on HMS *Nelson* is relatively simple, but on the French battleship *Richelieu* the main superstructure has eight levels and the platforms at each of the levels are shaped differently. Sometimes the problem is to decide on the underlying shape of the main superstructure to which the numerous platforms are attached. It is vital not to make any of the levels slightly too high because of the cumulative effect of such errors.

Platforms are made of two main parts, the horizontal base and the vertical sides. I make the base of wood, but if the shape is complex, it is best to make the base several times too thick and then sandpaper it to the correct thickness. If one attempts to shape a complex platform initially with a very thin piece of wood it is likely to break. It is also much simpler to make a complex platform in two parts, port and starboard, rather than make it in one piece. I use paper for the vertical sides of platforms, but it must be suitable. Some paper is too coarse and grainy, or too thin. The best paper that I have found is the glossy paper produced for loose-leaf stamp album pages. If the shape is complicated it is best not to use too long a piece of paper with, say, four to eight bends or angles. It is much easier to use several pieces of paper and never have more than one bend or angle in each. The paper only needs to be glued at the bottom, not the sides. Each piece is glued as close to the next as possible, and any minute vertical gaps can be sealed with paint.

Armament

I make one gun turret or mounting as accurately as possible and then mount this temporarily on a piece of wood and use it as a pattern for all the others. The temptation to glue the first turret into position on the model immediately should be resisted. Under 'Materials' above I have already referred to the use of tapered cocktail sticks for main and secondary armament. Great care should be taken in making turrets as some have up to fifteen angled surfaces. If the angles are not correct, the whole look of the completed model will seem wrong. I make the turret as a rectangular block initially, and then gradually work at the angled surfaces in the horizontal and vertical planes. The blast bags around the base of the guns of the main armament are made with polyfilla and then carved to shape with a scalpel.

Light AA guns need to be made on a 'production line' basis. The *Richelieu* has fourteen quadruple 40mm Bofors guns and my mountings and gun tubs each have fifteen parts, using wood, paper and wire. If making numerous mountings in one sitting seems too repetitive, make them in

(top)
The French battleship *Richelieu*, 1944/45.

(right)
The long and impressive forecastle of *Richelieu*. Note the main armament of eight 15in guns concentrated forward in two quadruple turrets. Given their radically different armament layouts, it is surprising to learn that *Richelieu* and *Tirpitz* were virtually identical in length and displacement.

Midships and stern of *Richelieu*, showing the three triple 6in turrets and the plethora of light AA guns fitted after her refit in the USA.

two or three batches, but always check with the initial pattern mounting for uniformity.

Funnels

After shaping the funnel I hollow it out, by cutting it in half lengthwise with a new double-edged razor blade to ensure a clean cut which will hardly be noticeable when reglued. A scalpel, needle file and sandpaper are used in hollowing out and the funnel can be very thin at the top but thicker at the base for strength. Any slight join when the funnel has been glued together again can usually be concealed by the vertical steampipes which are normally at the fore and aft ends of the funnel.

Most funnels have a steel grid or mesh at the top and this can be made from thin wire. Depending how closely spaced the pieces of the grid are, it is not always possible to fit the full number of pieces but this does not really matter. Even if the full number cannot be fitted, the top of the funnel will look much more realistic than it would with no grid at all.

The photographs of the *Richelieu* and the *Tone* show that these have complex funnel shapes and every attempt should be made to get them correct. A wrongly-shaped funnel can spoil an otherwise excellent model. Some warship funnels are vertical, but most are raked, and some are tapered. On the *Richelieu* only the bottom half is tapered.

Anchor Chain

I have not yet been able to produce a chain of linked pieces at 1:1250 scale, but I use a method which gives better results than a single length of wire or two pieces twisted together. I take a piece of fine wire and wrap it tightly around a thin pin to make a coil. Removing it from the pin I cut it into circular pieces with a scalpel which I paint by dropping these into some paint and then removing them. When dry these coils are glued to the deck in a line and this looks realistic.

Miscellaneous

I try to make as many minor fittings as possible, as these help to make the model look more authentic. The only exceptions are that I do not attempt wireless aerials (other than whip aerials) and wires running from masts or deck rails, because of the small scale. I once saw a photograph of a 1:1250 model warship with deck rails and although this was a valiant attempt, the rails were still over scale. Deck rails are not visible unless one is fairly close to the vessel. As much as possible of the minor equipment on the main deck should be modelled, and as this is often not shown in plans, close-up photographs of the deck are very useful.

One final point arises about the order of assembly. I always leave fragile parts that are likely to be damaged accidentally to as late a stage of assembly as possible. This principally means light AA guns, masts and mast fittings, but I did have problems with the tripod masts of the *Tone*, which I left to a late stage. I had difficulty in drilling the holes for these at the appropriate angles and I now realise that it would have been easier if I had done this earlier.

Painting

One must decide on the colour scheme before work starts as it is essential to paint as work progresses and it should not be left until the model is nearly complete. As far as possible I paint parts before they are glued, and then only touching-up should be needed later. I deal with very small parts by what I call 'reverse painting', *ie* dropping them into a small pool of paint and removing them with fine tweezers and putting the parts to dry. Wire should be left in the paint for a few minutes to give the paint an opportunity to adhere.

Once the hull has been painted I mount it temporarily with double-sided sellotape on a piece of wood as a base and it remains there until construction is completed. This avoids handling the model as constantly touching the hull leaves grease stains which are particularly noticeable if the paint scheme is a light grey. When the model is complete, a scalpel is used to separate it from the base and any sellotape remaining on the underside of the hull has to be removed carefully. Some paints need to be toned down. White is used normally for the blast bags around the base of the main armament, or as canvas covers on open boats. Adding a little light grey can tone this down and the colour still looks white on the model, but it is not too brilliant.

On the *Tone* I needed to make up a colour for the deck linoleum and after experiment I found that I needed to combine two colours in the proportions 11 to 10. If I need to make up another tin of the mixture I try the paint out on a piece of wood first to see that it matches the original. I have not referred to the two paints used as I have since discovered that I was using a somewhat inaccurately-coloured painting as a reference! Having recently obtained a colour chip of the Japanese deck linoleum, I have found that the Humbrol 160 Matt German camouflage Red-Brown is the correct colour to use for this.

I keep a notebook listing all the paints used on each model, which is very useful if the model should be damaged subsequently or if I need to use the same shade of grey on another model. It is surprising how quickly one can forget what colours were used.

Seas and Cases

When making the hull, I also shape another piece of wood with the hull form at the waterline, which I paint black or red as the case may be to reproduce the waterline or boot topping colour. I glue this on the base of the case before making the sea, and

when the sea has been built up around it, only a minute part of the black or red remains visible. The hull is then glued on top of this. The result is a very accurate straight line for the waterline.

I make my seas with Polyfilla, although other modellers use Plasticine, carved wood, a resin or other materials, and I shape this with a small spatula. As my dramatic bow waves on the *Roma* were not a great success, in more recent models I have always shown the vessel concerned proceeding at a moderate speed and in a light sea. I always try to use a photograph of the vessel in such conditions to reproduce the wake, as this can vary considerably from ship to ship.

I will conclude with two good tips which I have had from other modellers. Firstly, a model should have a reasonable amount of sea around it, and the sides of the case should not be so close to the model that it 'cannot breathe'. Secondly if for example the bows of the model are pointing to the left (taking the name plate

The Japanese heavy cruiser *Tone*. Japanese cruisers of this period were striking-looking vessels and rank high among modellers' favourite subjects - and not just in Japan.

(right)
Close-up of the *Tone*'s forecastle and superstructure. Note again the main armament concentrated forward.

as the front of the case) then the model should not be in the centre of the case but slightly to the right. The result is that the model appears to be steaming into the centre of the sea.

I have not commented on cases as I buy commercial cases, which are the only items I do not make.

The Models

I will not attempt to describe the models in detail, only first giving brief details of each ship and then describing any practical problems, which arose in construction, as these should be of general interest. The tonnage given is standard displacement, length is overall and the armament is the main armament. The model shows the vessel in a particular year and this is the date which follows the ship's name.

HMS *Nelson* 1943

(British battleship. Completed 1927, broken up 1948. 33,300 tons, 719ft and nine 16in guns. Extensive war service with the Home Fleet and in the Mediterranean.)

As my first Second World War battleship I chose HMS *Nelson* because of the simple 'block' superstructure, which was nicknamed ' Queen Anne's Mansions' after a block of flats. I also found the mid-war four-colour camouflage scheme attractive, but when the hull was painted, it was not easy to see the division between the light grey parts and the light blue/grey parts. I then painted a thin dark grey line on the dividing line between the two colours and although this did not exist in reality, it achieved the desired effect on the model.

K.M. *Tirpitz* 1944

(German battleship. Completed 1941, sunk 1944. 42,900 tons, 814ft and nine 15in guns. Spent most of the war in Norwegian fjords, attacked by British carrier aircraft, then by midget submarines and finally sunk by British bombers.)

The *Tirpitz* has a more complex superstructure than the *Nelson*, but few platforms. This was the first time that I had made light AA guns, but fortunately the numbers were small compared with American battleships. One aspect which was not a success was the diagonal black stripes, which formed part of the camouflage. These go in straight lines across the hull and up the turrets and superstructure, but on the model these do not always form continuous straight lines where these carry on up from the hull to the superstructure or turret. I realised that I should have marked the lines in pencil at a much earlier stage of construction, and these should have been painted before numerous small parts had been put in position.

Roma 1943

(Italian battleship. Completed 1942, sunk 1943. 40,990 tons, 789ft and nine 15in guns. *Roma*'s only claim to fame is that guided bombs from German bombers sank her, while on the way to surrender at Malta.)

I chose the *Roma* because she was a little known but handsome vessel with an attractive 'splinter' camouflage scheme. She posed two new problems. First, the main superstructure consisted of a narrow tapering cylindrical armoured tower, around which various platforms were fitted. Secondly, there were two large platforms above the level of the secondary armament on which most of the light AA guns are fitted. I constructed these with a wood base and paper sides (as described above) but at the time I had not realised that it was best to build the sides with numerous short pieces of paper rather than using fewer pieces with complex bends.

Despite being criticised for them, I am confident the bright red and white stripes on the forecastle and quarterdeck are correct. These were identification stripes to prevent Italian aircraft from attacking their own warships. I have photographs, which show that these stripes were kept in immaculate condition in wartime.

USS Alabama 1945

(American battleship. Completed 1942, preserved as a museum ship at Mobile, Alabama. 37,970 tons, 680ft and nine 16in guns. After convoy escort duty on Russian convoys, she took part in numerous engagements in the Pacific, including the battles of the Philippine Sea and Leyte Gulf.)

There were two main problems. First, the *Alabama* is a very compact ship, the whole tightly packed superstructure being only 2in long on the model. Secondly, in 1945 she had a very numerous light AA armament of twelve quadruple 40mm Bofors and fifty single 20mm Oerlikons. It was just a matter of making these on a 'production line' basis and trying not to be too discouraged by the repetitive work.

Another more minor problem was how to make the two catapults and the aircraft-handling crane. These were too small to make with wire on a girder basis, and yet painted wood would not have looked very realistic. In the end I used some soft clear plastic which was easy to shape and then painted the girders on it and the result looks reasonably realistic. I also spent considerable effort on the two tiny Curtiss Seahawk floatplanes, which have clear plastic cockpits and hand-painted five-point American stars. One of my frequent complaints is that I have seen a considerable number of otherwise excellent warship models in museums and exhibitions, which are spoilt by inaccurate and poorly-made aircraft which it would have been better to omit.

IJN Kitakami 1941

(Japanese torpedo cruiser. Completed 1921. Broken up 1947. 5100 tons and forty 24in torpedo tubes. Built as a light cruiser, 1941 converted to a torpedo cruiser, 1942-3 converted to carry landing craft and in 1945 to carry eight midget submarines.)

My idea was to make a relatively simple model as a change from making battleships. This was not entirely successful as after completion I realised that as much

detailed work as possible should be put into an otherwise simple model.

Richelieu 1944/5

(French battleship. Completed 1940. Broken up 1964. 35,000 tons, 813ft and eight 15in guns. Attacked by British at Dakar 1940, later went over to the Free French Forces, refitted in the United States and in 1944/5 served with the British Eastern Fleet in the Indian Ocean.)

This is my most complex model involving over 1000 hours work and having nearly 1600 parts. Because she was a relatively little-known vessel it took me six years to collect the information to make to model. I was attracted to the *Richelieu* because she was a powerful-looking vessel and also had a peculiarly angled combined funnel and aft superstructure.

There were three main problems. The chief one was the main superstructure, which had a considerable number of deck levels most with projecting platforms all of different shapes. The next was the numerous light AA armament, which was similar to the *Alabama* because of *Richelieu*'s refit in the United States, except that there were fourteen quadruple 40mm Bofors to make! In the case of both the main superstructure and the AA armament, it was mainly a matter of slogging. Because of the numerous deck levels the main superstructure needed constant checking to ensure that it was not gradually getting too tall. Another more minor problem was the two platforms near the funnel on which the heavy AA guns were fitted. Each platform was a complex irregular shape and the vertical sides had sixteen different facets. I solved this by using twelve pieces of paper for the sides of each platform. The final problem was painting a straight line for the division between the light blue and the light grey camouflage on the hull at main deck level. As my initial attempt at painting this freehand was not satisfactory, I tried using masking tape and I was surprised that it worked at such a small scale. I pressed it on firmly, no paint seeped underneath it and when removing it no paint underneath was pulled off.

An innovation was a flag at the stern, made of paper. Some flags on models look like rigid boards and I wanted to avoid this. Apart from drooping the flag a little, I also crinkled it somewhat, when viewed from above. This needed to be done several times as the crinkles are inclined to unfold. Finally I cut a minute triangle off each of the trailing edges. This is another example of doing something on a model, which does not exist on the real ship, yet helps to make the model realistic.

Tone 1944

(Japanese heavy cruiser. Completed 1938. Sunk 1945. Broken up 1948. 11,215 tons, 650ft and eight 8in guns. 1941 part of the Pearl Harbor Task Force. Later she took part in numerous engagements in the Pacific and Indian Oceans and the battles of Midway 1942 and Leyte Gulf 1944.)

I was attracted to Japanese heavy cruisers as they were striking-looking vessels which were about as complex as a battleship, but on a much narrower beam. Comparing the *Alabama*, which was a rather small battleship, with the *Tone*, the *Alabama* had a length of 680ft and a beam of 108ft, whereas the dimensions for the *Tone* were 650ft and 61ft respectively. The *Tone* had her main armament of eight 8in guns in four turrets forward and the aft superstructure and quarterdeck had catapults, rails and turntables for handling

and storing up to six reconnaissance floatplanes.

One unusual item I have not had to tackle before was the four quadruple torpedo tubes which are recessed in the upper deck. I had to leave two rectangular spaces in the upper deck for the torpedo tubes, which I then fitted. After that I had to make a thin deck to cover them in, and plate the sides, after carving the appropriate recesses. As is to be expected of Japanese naval architecture, all four recesses on each side were different shapes and sizes!

The main problem was the catapult floatplanes and I decided to make four, two Mitsubishi 'Pete' single float biplanes and two Aichi 'Jake' twin float monoplanes. The model 'Petes' which were smaller, only had a wingspan of 8.5mm. I found the chief difficulty was not making the small parts, but gluing them on, as in the process I often knocked off other parts. After several attempts and almost giving up, I was glad that I had persevered. The floatplanes took 50 hours work and they are colourful as they have six colours. As warships are generally rather drab, it is always worth considering what other small items of colour can legitimately can be added to a model for interest.

Conclusion

This chapter follows two chapters on making large-scale models of HMS *Glorious* and HMS *Hood*. Techniques obviously do

Tone's after quarterdeck and aircraft catapult arrangements, from above. Simulating water convincingly is a challenge to any modeller.

differ depending on the scale of the model but one cardinal rule applies irrespective of scale and that is the model should be as accurate as possible. A fallacy relating to miniatures is that an error or inaccuracy will not be so obvious as the model is so small. The answer is that as the model is built to scale, an error or inaccuracy will still show despite the small size.

Making miniature warships is a fascinating and rewarding hobby, both in researching the vessel and in constructing it. Miniatures have the additional advantage that there is no storage problem at home, unlike large scale warship models. The two most important matters to decide at the outset are (1) that one has more than adequate information in the way of plans and photographs and (2) the date of the model. At an early stage of construction, I decide what my next model will be, so that I am simultaneously working on one model and researching the next.

A modeller should develop his skills and techniques over a period of time, and while a model should always present some sort of challenge, it is best not to be over ambitious otherwise disappointment may result. I have yet to tackle a Japanese battleship of the *Fuso*, *Ise* or *Nagato* classes, which with their massive and extremely complicated superstructures, seem the ultimate challenge in Second World War warship models.

A modeller can always learn from other modellers. When I made HMS *Nelson*, I thought that it would be too difficult to make light AA guns, but having seen excellent light AA guns on another model battleship, I put these on my next model, the *Tirpitz*. If one wants to criticise another model, always try to remember that any comments should be constructive or helpful, not destructive. Some modellers seem to forget that modelmaking is a hobby, which should be enjoyable. In the same vein, do not be too disgruntled if one does not gain the highest award in a model competition, whether there are good reasons for this or not!

Always remember that other modellers can obtain excellent results by using different techniques or methods. While one should always paint woods along the grain and not across it, for most things in modelling there are usually several different methods which can all be equally satisfactory. It all depends on the individual modeller. I have found that the solution to many modelling problems can be simple, the only difficulty is that it might take several years to find that simple solution!

6
Model Warships from Plastic Kits

BY LOREN PERRY

Beginning in the early part of the twentieth century, model kits of various types began appearing on the market for the pleasure of ordinary consumers. Among the first such kits were replicas of famous fighting ships of both sail and steam powered varieties. These mostly wood and paper offerings provided the basic materials and a sheet of instructions with which to fabricate a reasonably detailed scale model of a well-known vessel.

But they still required a great deal of skill from the builder. Hulls had to be built or carved to final shape, small boats needed to be whittled from solid blocks, and any fine detailing usually required some scratchbuilding experience, at least until cast metal fittings came along. Because even the best kits demanded quite a bit of talent from their builders, sales were not high enough to warrant large investments by manufacturers in new products, and the range tended to be restricted to just a few major warships such as battleships, aircraft carriers, and maybe a submarine or two.

By 1950 injection plastic moulding had become available to larger model companies like Revell and Airfix. This process greatly simplified the work of the consumer-hobbyist; scratchbuilding experience was no longer a prerequisite for creating a well-shaped replica of a warship. These skills were now demanded only of the master patternmaker, and the science of mould-making made his work equally available to anyone with a little pocket money to spend at the toy or hobby store.

With the appearance of commercially available plastic kits, model ship sales began to skyrocket. Manufacturers now had the motivation to increase the size and variety of their ranges. Buyers (at first, mostly boys) began to build and collect entire fleets of miniature warships. By the 1980s, aftermarket suppliers were supporting the available kits with specialised products such as photoetched (PE) metal superdetails, decals, and prototype references. One of the first of these suppliers was Gold Medal Models, a maker of PE brass and stainless steel detail sets, many of which are specifically geared to particular kits. These detail sets enable average hobbyists to convert ordinary plastic kits into virtual works of art with a level of detail rivaling better scratchbuilt models. Today, many plastic kit builders often graduate to larger and more complex projects such as scratchbuilding museum-grade display miniatures and radio-controlled operating

Revell's 1:429 scale USS *Arizona*, showing the battleship as she appeared in 1934. A simulated drydock style display base made from small wooden blocks helps convey a sense of mass.

The *Arizona* again, this time converted into a waterline display model and shown as she was at Pearl Harbor on 7 December 1941.

scale models. But this chapter is about building from plastic kits, so let us restrict our attention to this subject for now.

Plastic model ship kits range in quality from simple toys for young children up to massive and elaborately detailed replicas of HMS *Victory*, complete with fully equipped lower gun decks and accurate rigging. The largest number of plastic warship builders tend to concentrate on steam-powered men-o'-war from the twentieth century, and especially the Second World War. Here, the variety is almost endless. Kits made from traditional injection moulded styrene plastic as well as the newer polymer resins cover almost all navies and a wide-ranging selection of ship types. Even auxiliary vessels have become popular with collectors as have lesser fighting ships like corvettes and patrol vessels. No longer an exclusive realm of young boys, plastic model shipbuilding has evolved into a highly sophisticated exercise in preserving military history for both men and women in countries around the world. The relatively inexpensive and quick to build nature of plastic model ship kits offers other benefits. For example, they permit amateur students of naval architecture to indulge themselves in replicating numerous camouflage schemes, assorted radar fits, and evolutions in armament, often using

duplicates of the same kit as their foundations, a luxury that was not at all practical for modelers of earlier times.

It is almost a paradox that some of the best plastic ship kits available today also happen to be some of the oldest. A prominent example is the famous Revell kit of the battleship USS *Arizona* produced in 1:429 scale. Why such an odd scale, instead of 1:400 or 1:600? The reason is that in the 1950s, when the *Arizona* kit was designed and released, manufacturers scaled their kits to fit into standard-sized cardboard boxes. This decision was based on a desire to assist the hobby store owners of that era in stacking their kit boxes in tidy rows on shelves. If they were all the same size, the job was greatly simplified.

Airfix was one of the first manufacturers to produce kits in standarized scales, such as 1:600, a wise decision that promoted collecting. The advantage of this approach produced correct-size relationships between models of large and small warship types whereas the 'box-scale' idea tended to make all warship types more or less the same size, typically between 1 and 2ft in length. While today's manufacturers still have not settled on a universal series of standard scales, a few of the smaller scales do seem to have attracted a substantial following. Some of them include 1:600, 1:400, 1:350, and

SAMPLE INSTRUCTION ARTWORK

REMOVING PLASTIC RAILING

The following parts in Revell's USS *Arizona* kit must have their molded plastic railing and/or molded inclined ladders removed: 2 and 3 (Hull Halves), 10 (Superstructure Deck), 15 (Aft Deck), 19 (Emergency Cabin Platform), 20 (Flag Bridge), 21 (Catwalk), 22 (Navigation Bridge), 23 (Range Finder Platform), 40 (Mainmast Searchlight Platform), 43 (Mainmast Range Finder Platform), and 49 (Foremast Machine Gun Platform). CAUTION: On Parts 20, 22, and 23, remove only those areas that represent an open-type railing. These areas have a raised horizontal ribbing effect on their outer surfaces. Leave all other bulwarks intact.

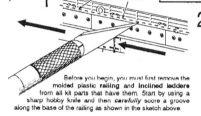

1 Score a groove along the dotted line.

Before you begin, you must first remove the molded plastic railing and inclined ladders from all kit parts that have them. Start by using a sharp hobby knife and then *carefully* score a groove along the base of the railing as shown in the sketch above.

2

Once all the rails have been scored, *gently* bend the molded railing back and forth until it breaks free. Use a chisel-shaped hobby knife blade to remove molded inclined ladders.

3

NOTE: It may be easier to use only a file and sandpaper on some of the smaller parts instead of scoring and breaking the railing off.

Use a flat file to level the upper surface. It must be as flat and even as possible so that the etched brass railing will fit properly. Clean up the surface with fine sandpaper.

FIGHTING TOPS

NOTE: File away molded plastic window frames before assembling fighting tops.

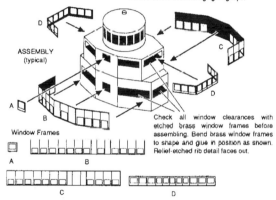

ASSEMBLY (typical)

Window Frames

A   B

C

D

Check all window clearances with etched brass window frames before assembling. Bend brass window frames to shape and glue in position as shown. Relief-etched rib detail faces out.

HATCHES

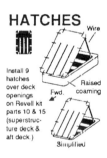

Wire

Install 9 hatches over deck openings on Revell kit parts 10 & 15 (superstructure deck & aft deck.)

Raised coaming

Fwd.

Simplified

AIRCRAFT DETAILS

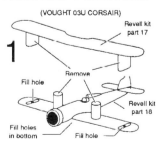

(VOUGHT 03U CORSAIR)

1

Revell kit part 17

Remove

Fill hole

Revell kit part 18

Fill holes in bottom

Fill hole

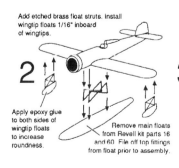

2

Add etched brass float struts. Install wingtip floats 1/16" inboard of wingtips.

Apply epoxy glue to both sides of wingtip floats to increase roundness.

Remove main floats from Revell kit parts 16 and 60. File off top fittings from float prior to assembly.

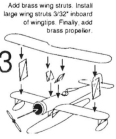

3

Add brass wing struts. Install large wing struts 3/32" inboard of wingtips. Finally, add brass propeller.

Sample instruction artwork from a plastic kit.

now 1:700, the latter almost exclusively devoted to 'waterline' modelling *ie* with no underwater details. There are literally hundreds of kits available of all types of warship, so modern ship modelers will have little difficulty finding something that appeals to them.

Newer kits by large manufacturers are much improved over early offerings. The parts count is often larger and shapes are more accurate, with improved detailing being the norm. Some of the better kits approach museum-grade accuracy and even offer various options such as early or late equipment fits.

Photoetched Details

The basic process of building a plastic kit is familiar to almost all ship modelers. Advanced builders have developed techniques to bring out the best in these mass-produced products, giving them more of an individual hand-made look. Adding photoetched details has become one of the most popular ways of refining a plastic

warship kit. PE accessories offer the modeler a great deal of options such as a huge variety of radar antennas, watertight doors, details for on-board aircraft, and even tiny 3-D figures for use in dioramas.

Photoetched detailing became popular in the late 1980s and several manufacturers now offer products in almost any scale one can imagine. Some are designed to enhance existing plastic kits while others are included with resin model kits. Because these parts are made of lightweight sheet metal, builders can learn to use these parts by employing methods akin to those used with paper or card models. Obviously, PE fittings will not respond to the usual plastic solvent cements, so a different type of adhesive is needed. Cyanoacrylate (CA) glues are among the most widely used types, but a few hobbyists prefer white glue which can be brushed on and cleaned up with tap water. If the model is made of styrene and has not been painted yet, items like watertight doors can be secured with liquid solvent-type cement. The cement softens the plastic enough to grip the door,

Etched brass railings, ladders and other details are available for a wide range of kits.

Larger-scale models, such as this 1:200 Japanese destroyer by Nichimo allow the modeller to indulge in even higher levels of detailing. The photoetched railings even show an etched-in 'sag' in their simulated chains.

and a coat of paint further strengthens the bond. In fact, some modelers successfully use paint to hold very small items like doors. PE parts do not need any primer before painting or gluing provided they are clean and free of greasy fingerprints.

Plastic modelers have also perfected the art of illusion when detailing their smaller models. For example, the effect of a wooden planked deck can be simulated on a plastic ship's deck by brushing streaks of several different-coloured stains over a previously applied coat of light tan paint. By keeping the streaks the width of a plank or two, the final effect can be very convincing. It has even been shown that careful masking and airbrushing of varying shades of gray paint can produce the appearance of a rippled steel skin on a warship's hull. The airbrushed shading can be so convincing that a viewer will often be compelled to carefully run his or her fingertips along the side of the hull to 'feel' the depressions that are not really there at all.

How a model is built is also dictated by the way it is going to be displayed. If destined for a traditional museum-type display case, the warship in question will generally be finished in a pristine, spotless manner with no figures, all doors and

hatches closed, and all guns and radars centered, while ships that will be part of a diorama will normally display heavily 'weathered' exteriors, figures on the upper decks, and guns, doors, and other equipment in random positions. And it is not unusual for 1:700 naval crewmembers to boast fully detailed uniforms, or to be displayed in vignettes aboard ship that actually tell a story. Clearly, one will have to think about this early on before actually proceeding with the model's construction.

Older modelers (and a few younger ones) have come to depend on magnifying lenses, especially those worn on the head like hoods, when building in the smaller scales. Tweezers of several types are also indispensable as are tools common to professions such as dentistry and even surgery. It is amazing what the modern plastic ship modeler can achieve these days, and it is little wonder that so many of them are winning gold medals and Best of Show awards in competitions around the world.

Some model builders will convert larger scale models to a waterline display by carefully sawing off the underwater hull. An aircraft carrier makes an attractive subject for such a conversion; depicting full flight operations on the flight deck looks odd when the model is displayed on a miniature drydock base inside a glass case. Simulating the water for large warships is fairly easy. A sheet of rippled clear plastic makes for a good 'sea' after its smooth underside has been painted blue. Artists'

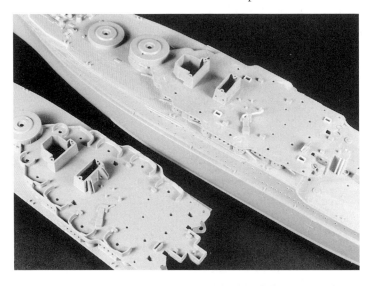

modelling putty is easy to apply and sculpt into bow waves and wakes after which they can be painted white. The ship can simply be glued or screwed down to the 'sea' with modeler's paste built up lightly around the edges to blend it in. For more lively seas with lots of wave action, various modeling putties available at art supply stores are available. A hint - practice your wave-making technique on some scrap material before committing yourself to your finished model.

The difference between an ordinary plastic model warship and a very good one depends on how much time the builder is willing to invest in it. For example, injection-moulded plastic parts are pushed from their moulds by ejector pins that leave marks on the plastic components. These should be filled and sanded until invisible. 'Flash' is excess plastic seen around the edges of parts and caused by ill-fitting

(above)
Preparing a plastic warship kit for detailing often requires the removal of moulded-on details. The upper deck of this kit (left) displays overly-thick splinter shields and unrealistic ladders. At right, the same deck after these offending items have been cut away. PE and/or sheet plastic replacements will be fitted instead.

(right)
Before-and-after views of a gun-turret aircraft catapult. The heavy plastic part supplied in the kit is replaced with a much improved and far more detailed PE version.

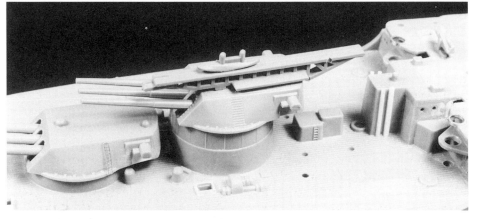

Extra-fine railings and ladders from the Gold Metal Models PE detail set help make older plastic models much more convincing replicas of the originals.

Rigging plastic models is often done with 'invisible thread', a very thin nylon monofilament sold at fabric shops. On this model, the rigging has been painted light gray, enabling it to be seen better in photographs. Normally it would be left natural, providing a more true-to-scale appearance. Stretched plastic sprue is also a favourite material for rigging.

mould halves. This must be carefully trimmed away and sanded smooth to ensure a good fit for adjacent parts. Sink marks - small depressions caused by sudden cooling of newly-moulded plastic components - should be filled with putty or thick CA glue and sanded smooth. Sometimes an affected part will have its engraved detailing disrupted by one or more of these flaws. In the case of a simulated planked deck, the detailing can be restored after the flaws are corrected by carefully re-engraving the lost planks into the surface with a sharp hobby knife using a small straightedge as a guide. Once painted, the problem area becomes almost invisible. If it still shows, a clever modeller can often hide the flaw with a few figures or bits of equipment placed judiciously.

Plastic masts that come with most kits are usually too thick or rendered in an overly simple manner, so many advanced modelers will replace them with duplicates constructed of thin brass wire or bits of heat-stretched plastic sprue (this is made from the plastic frames, or runners, that hold all the parts of a kit together when manufactured). Brass replacements are superior because yardarms and braces can be rendered in a much closer-to-scale thickness while maintaining, or even surpassing, the original parts' strength. This is especially important when rigging a model, because thin plastic masts will often bend or deform when tension is applied to the rigging. Furthermore, if a model is subjected to temperature extremes, the rigging will probably expand or contract, adding additional stress to the masts. Brass parts are excellent insurance against this problem.

Applying decals is common among plastic kits. They might represent underwater draft marks, hull pendant numbers, deck warning stripes, or even markings on shipboard aircraft. The most commonly seen problem with conventional waterslide decals is 'silvering'. This is the silvery-white 'fog' that sometimes appears on a dried decal after it has been applied to a finished model, usually caused by a matte-painted surface to which the decal has been applied. Microscopic air bubbles become trapped within the rough surface of a matte finish and the decal film seals them in, making them visible in the form of silvering. To prevent this, the area to be decaled should be finished in a glossy paint, or treated with a clear gloss overcoat. A gentle blotting with a soft clean cloth now allows the air bubbles to escape. Once the decal has dried, a clear flat coat can be applied, preferably with an airbrush, which will restore the uniform matte finish.

Displaying the Model

Display bases can add tremendously to a plastic model's visual appeal. Museum models and official builders' models are often mounted on heavy wooden plinths with a scale representation of drydock blocks under the hull. This type of display hints at a great weight being supported and gives the model a feeling of mass and substance, while also being a very attractive way to present the model to viewers. Such a display is best used with replicas of large vessels such as battleships, cruisers, and aircraft carriers, but smaller ships like destroyers can also benefit. Another type of display employs turned brass pedestals. Normally, four are required: two located fore and aft along the keel, the other two located amidships under the sides of the hull to stabilize the model. The pair on the keel should be spaced so they are about 25 per cent of the hull's length from each end. If they are any closer together, the model will look somewhat odd due to the excessive overhang at the ends. The pedestals can be custom turned on a lathe or made from decorative finials for table lamps. The latter can be purchased at hardware stores. One can even use highly-polished lengths of plain brass tubing cut to length - these can be quite attractive in their very simplicity as well as an economical alternative for modelers on a budget.

A custom nameplate is the finishing touch for a fine ship model, no matter what the model is made of. The nameplate can be computer generated using traditional

(bottom left)
Placing a model in a diorama allows it to tell a story. The sailors shown lined up for inspection in this Pearl Harbor diorama emphasise the suprise nature of the air attack on 7 December 1941.

(bottom right)
Detailing the masts of a Second World War or later warship can be demanding, but it adds greatly to the finished model's appeal. Tamiya's 1:350 scale *Fletcher* class destroyer displays its radars, jamming antennas and various communications equipment, all provided by a commercially-available PE set. Note also the PE sights and guardrails on the lighter guns.

Fine detail is also possible in 1:700 scale thanks again to commercial PE detail sets and stretched plastic sprue. The straps holding the folded liferafts in place are simply cut from light grey decal material and applied after the model has been painted. Dashed black decal stripes are used to simulate the scuppers in the bulwark on the main deck.

lettering fonts with an overall design similar to those used on official builders' models. White lettering on a black background with a white trimmed border is a most attractive combination. Choose fonts that are contemporaries of the vessel being represented, *ie* do not use ultra-modern lettering for a vessel from the Second World War. The nameplate is best located either amidships or near the bow of the model, traditionally on the ship's starboard side. One can also make two plates for viewing of either side. If the ship is enclosed in a glass case, the nameplate should be inside the case.

Photography

Photographing your model is a good way to maintain a record of your work. To make your 'official portraits', choose a medium-coloured sheet of heavy paper from your art supply store, or cloth from a fabric shop. A medium blue, green, or gray are all good choices. Black is also acceptable for dramatic photos, but the model will have to be carefully illuminated to show the darker details such as black painted mast tops or rigging.

Your camera must be capable of exposing film with very small aperture sizes in its lens. If the aperture is too large (such

as f.2.8 or f.4), some of the model will be out of focus. Settings of f.16 or greater (higher numbers equal smaller apertures) will keep more of your model in focus, especially when shooting three-quarter views of the ship's entire length. Always use the smallest aperture setting your camera is capable of. Smaller apertures require strong lighting and longer exposure times, so you may want to invest in a tripod to steady the camera for razor-sharp images. A couple of inexpensive portable floodlights will also allow you to photograph indoors whenever you want. Without floodlights, you will have to shoot outdoors on a slightly hazy day to prevent harsh shadows. In any case,

This 1:700 scale Japanese aircraft carrier displays a full air wing of highly-detailed miniature aircraft, complete with propellers, landing gear and markings, all available today from aftermarket suppliers. The elaborate camouflage scheme is also noteworthy.

A neat paint job, delicate railings and realistically drooping flags all add to a plastic model's final appearance. By mimicking the features of traditional builders' models, a plastic kit can capture some of the visual impact of a finely-crafted museum piece at a fraction of the cost in both time and money.

your background must be plain and without visual distraction. This also includes the immediate foreground.

Lighting a model is the trickiest part of tabletop photography. Remember to light the entire length of a ship model so that the bow or stern does not appear darker than the centre. When focusing, pick a spot about one-third back from the closest part of the model and focus on that. The camera will be able to keep the forward third and rear two-thirds of the model in sharper focus if you remember this trick. One final note: remember that a plastic model is particularly vulnerable to high temperatures, so keep your lights off until you are ready to shoot. And do not forget the rigging - heat will shrink it tight.

Conclusion

Building plastic warship kits can be a springboard to more complex forms of ship modelling or they can be a unique art form in their own right. Many highly skilled scratchbuilders enjoy relaxing with a good kit and yet will take the time to employ some photoetched detailing or other techniques to make their models just a bit better. No matter how one views a plastic model ship kit, the fact is they are here to stay and their quality is improving with each passing year. As time goes by, they will continue to introduce thousands of people, both young and old, to the satisfaction of replicating great fighting ships in miniature.

7
Working Model Small Craft: Sub-chaser *SC 1055*

BY DAVID JACK

It can take a long time to scratch-build a model; often the research can take longer than the actual building, assuming the information you need is available. As my main interest is around the era of the Second World War a lot of information is not readily available any more: some photograph collections have been bought by private collectors, and I know some of the commercial photographers with long association to the Admiralty have destroyed some of their negatives. Ex-servicemen can be an excellent source of photographs, but as time marches on their numbers inevitably decrease. The usual archive sources have vast stocks of photographs but I think the majority are not catalogued, so unless you can visit the archives yourself you will be limited by what time the archivist can spare you.

Generally I have long had the same maritime interests, so for many years I have accumulated articles, photographs, books, and anything that relates to small mostly wooden-built naval craft, be they ASRLs, MTBs or MLS. I may be a bit of a magpie but often it pays off in the end.

Drawings can be another problem. They can usually be obtained from the shipbuilders or if they have gone out of business their drawings are often passed on to the nearest university or library (in Britain, also the Imperial War Museum or the National Maritime Museum). Also numerous advertised sources such as John Lambert can provide them. There are often good drawings available in other countries as well, such as France, the US, Germany,

Poland etc. For access to these you can use either the Internet, foreign magazines or if you can get to any of the model shows around the world, the publishers will often have stands there. These drawings are of mixed quality but usually quite good. It should be noted that quite often photographs and research will cost more than the materials to build the model.

Personally my choice of subject usually stems from a photograph or an article which grabs my imagination. I look into it to see if there is much information available, and if it looks hopeful, then I will pursue all available sources which can take years. I do have a list of subjects I want to build and as I finish one model I am thinking of the next. If I do not have enough information I will put it back a bit until I feel I have got all that is available on it. I try to model a boat at a particular time in its life, usually determined by the photographs. Often there is a group of on-completion photos available or a newspaper or war photographer can take a batch of shots. These are ideal and often dated.

SC 1055

I liked the look of the sub-chaser and as I had already built the approximate British and German equivalents (the Fairmile 'B' and the Raüm boat) I felt it was an attractive craft and references seemed to be available.

I usually work in ½in =1ft (1:24) scale as it is a good size for sailing while

The completed model
of *SC 1055*.

Another of the
author's models, an
80ft Elco PT Boat.

also large enough to get an MTB or PT
Boat to work successfully. At 110ft long
with an 18ft 7¾in beam the sub-chaser
compared well to the Fairmile 'B' and
Raüm boat, with similar performance
figures. The model came in at 55in
(1400mm) long.

I think the majority of these vessels
were used in the Pacific, where operations
were of a different nature to the European
War, but some operated in the
Mediterranean, and others from the British
Isles and off the US Coast, in convoy escort
and general service duties.

They were based on a 1917 110ft

design, which was very successful during
the First World War, of which 440 were
built. When the outbreak of the Second
World War appeared imminent, the US
Navy realised they would require a craft to
do a similar job and eventually this design
was chosen at a cost of $325,000 each. The
later sub-chaser was a much improved and
beamier design but apparently still
infamous for its tendency to roll.

SC 1055 did not have a spectacular
history. She was launched on 10 October
1942 and commissioned on 10 May 1943.
She was transferred to the Coast Guard on
27 November 1945 and was decommissioned
on 5 April 1946, then sold on 15 June
1948. I managed to get some excellent 'on
completion' photographs of her from the
USA, taken both onboard and on trials off
Wilmington California from most angles.
With the aid of a magnifying glass I was
able to get most of the finer details, some of
which were unclear on the drawings.

The US National Archives were able
to supply some of the photos of *1055*; I
also got some from Real War Photos in the
US, taken at the same time. I also
remembered a documentary on the
television some years ago about the
'Shetland Bus', when Norwegian fishermen

ran an escape route from Norway and dropped agents and supplies for Resistance during the Second World War. I recalled there was a sub-chaser up on stocks in Norway. I wrote to the embassy and they put me in touch with the commanding officer who was very helpful providing me with copies of drawings and photographs, even including copies of the blueprints.

One of only seven hulls left afloat in the world, the *Hitra* was one of three sub-chasers supplied in August 1943. They helped supply Norwegian agents, as they had taken some grievous losses in 1942-3 using fishing boats. Admiral Nimitz became aware of the problem and with President Roosevelt's approval the US supplied three sub-chasers, *SC 683* (*Hessa*), *SC 1061* (*Vigra*) and *SC 718* (*Hitra*). They made a tremendous difference due to their speed and ability to defend themselves. The *Hitra* and her sisters were decommissioned in 1957 and sold in 1959 for 1 Krona each. *Hessa* and *Vigra* are no more but in 1981 a Russian 'Whisky' class submarine ran aground off Karlskrona in Sweden. Nearby part of a bow protruded out of the water, and this was the *Hitra*. Her last commanding officer, now commander of the Norwegian naval museum, went to look at it and confirmed it was her. The

chief of the Royal Norwegian Navy founded 'the Friends of *Hitra*', with funds raised and a lot of goodwill she was raised and transported to Oma shipyard in Norway in 1983. By 1987 the restoration was completed. She is now a sailing museum and tours the Norwegian coast each summer and makes occasional trips to the Shetlands.

As the excellent Al Ross's drawings of *1474* for the dimensions and the photographs of *1055* were available - for the detail - I modelled that one. Anyone building a US warship really is very fortunate, as there is an abundance of photos available. They also tend to photograph every modification, so with good quality drawings and excellent photographs I felt I was ready to start.

Building the Model

Hull

I first took a tracing of the keel and traced that onto a sheet of 6mm brunzeal marine plywood, cutting it out with a power fretsaw. Using a tenon saw I made a saw cut vertically in the bow approximately 20mm deep following the line of the stem. I then bonded a piece of brass 1mm x 22mm into

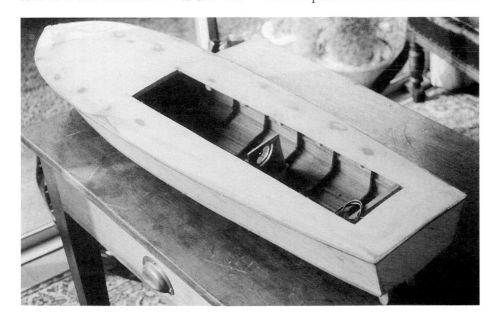

The hull of the PT boat, sanded and ready for painting.

the cut with araldite leaving 2mm proud down the stem. This gives the bow some strength in case of a sailing accident.

Then the frames were photocopied and cut out of paper and stuck down to 6mm plywood and again cut out with the fretsaw leaving a flat top edge. After that a notch is cut out of the bottom of each frame for the keel. The frames are checked on the keel for alignment with my finger on the edge and pencil in hand. I ran a pencil mark round the frame approximately 10mm in from the edge allowing a slightly larger gusset on each side of the keel for strength and rounded corners and the deck edge. The inside is then cut out with a miniature jigsaw. After checking they line up on the keel, I removed them and clamped them together to mark the line where the stringers will go. On a boat this size and hull shape, about six or seven per side including the ones alongside the keel and the deck edge are enough. Then using the Dremel fretsaw I cut 4mm square notches in each frame where each stringer goes on a smaller boat if weight is critical I would use 2mm or 3mm stringers.

I use an old wooden mantelpiece as a building board. At the frame spacings I use a set square to keep the frames at right angles to the keel and mark with a pencil where each frame goes on to the board, with the spacings taken from the drawing. I clamp each frame down vertically by temporarily screwing two pieces of 25mm square wood one on each side. Making sure the keel fits well and is straight, it is glued into the frames with PVA and left overnight.

Next the 4mm stringers are fitted; these are cut on a circular saw from timber or sometimes plywood, which works quite well. These are fitted on each side alternately, checking the keel is straight at intervals, again with PVA glue. Once left for a day it can be removed from the board, and the last two can be fitted to the deck edges, after removing the excess from the frames. The ends of the stringer are trimmed and if necessary balsa blocks are used to build up the bow and the stern depending on the shape. Once the glue is dry, it can all be sanded to shape, constantly checking that the shape is correct. I usually plank the hull horizontally with 1.8mm x 5mm obechi planks bought from the model shop, as they bend easily and are easy to sand. Glued with PVA and temporarily pinned, once the glue has dried the pins are removed, usually leaving the planks short of the brass stem by 2 or 3mm.

At this stage I cover the hull with 48mm masking tape and the inside is coated with glassfibre resin reinforced with nappy liners rather than glass cloth as they are lighter and do not take as much resin as the cloth does, saving a bit of weight. When the resin is gelled but not set I pull the tape off; it is only there to stop the resin running through. After a day it is dry enough to sand down. I use 40 grit paper to start with as I want it to cut through the high bits not round them over. Any filling required is done at this stage though it should not need much, and once satisfied, the outside is given a coat of glassfibre resin only, to seal the planks as obechi is very porous. After a light sand-down it is ready for the outside planking. At this stage the prop tubes and rudder shafts were trial fitted. I make sure the bow is not too thick either side of the brass as once the second layer is put on it can build up and look rounded and blunt.

Assuming an average plank of wood is around 2-3m, if I can see where the joints are on a photograph that can give a clue as to how long the planks would be. I then cut 1mm ply into 5mm by whatever length the planks are strips.

The sub-chaser is horizontally planked so I started from the edge of the deck, fixing them with impact glue and working alternately from side to side down to the waterline, then again alternately from the keel upwards. The planks are butted up against the brass in the bow, not onto it, so that once the planks are sanded smooth the brass can be filed down to leave a fine sharp bow.

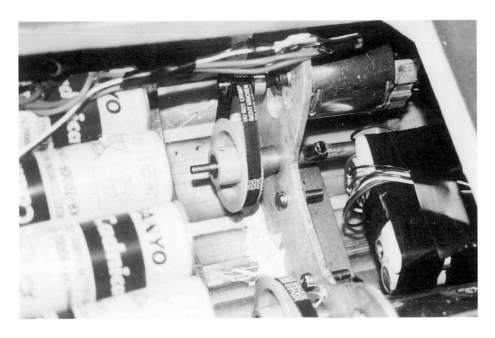

The motor and bulkhead setup on the sub-chaser. Note the battery pack for the lights (right).

After a good sanding-down and any minor filling is done, the prop tubes and rudder stems are fitted with araldite and any filling necessary is done round the prop tubes. It is easier this way as there is only one layer of 1mm ply to cut through as they have been trial fitted already. I usually use commercial brass rudders, which come with a rudder tube in plastic and a tiller arm. I cut them to shape and fill and sand them to the correct profile.

Motors

I would normally try the motor/battery set up now before I put the deck on to get the balance right. It is often critical for balance where the batteries go on coastal forces' boats.

Over the last few years I have been gearing the motors using toothed belts and pulleys. This has worked very well letting the motor run at its most efficient speed but with less drag on various types of boats. To do this I cut an aluminium bulkhead

Propeller shaft assembly and rudders on the sub-chaser.

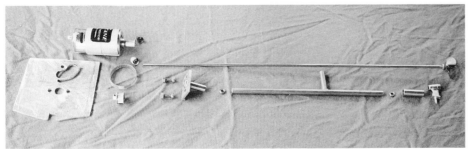

Propeller shaft and motor mount from the PT Boat.

3mm thick, mark where the propshaft will come through, and measure where the motor would be, making sure the deck or fitting would not be in the way. (The motors do not have to be directly above the shaft. They can be canted to one side or the other.) If I think the gearing should be, say, 2.5-1, depending on the speed of the motor and volts carried and size of prop I would make a card template with adjustment for the motors so I can change pulleys thus altering the gear ratio. They are large props so they need not run as fast as a smaller prop. I now make my own prop shafts with stainless ball bearing races at each end.

First I make two sleeves to take the bearings; the outer one is turned on the lathe with an inner collar for the bearing to butt against. The inner sleeve mounts on the other end of the prop tube also with an inner collar for the bearing but also with an outer collar to be soldered on to a piece of brass angle which is bolted to the aluminium bulkhead so the prop tube is held at a right angle to the bulkhead to ensure that the belts run true.

The bearings can take the sideways load due to the pull of the belts and also the shaft can run very freely with minimum drag. I slide the prop tube into the sleeves with some grease to keep water out. The outer collar is the only piece fixed and bonded into the hull. All the bearings, prop tube etc can be taken apart easily this way.

Depending on what height the inner end of the prop tube is, sometimes water can get past the bearings, but a small 'o' ring on the outside next to the bearing cures this. After trials and trying varying pulley combinations to check that everything is basically okay and there are no major problems, it is time to think about the deck.

Decks

To do this I glue a 10mm x 20mm balsa block to the side of each frame. Once dry it is sanded to shape to accommodate the camber on the deck, checking by eye. Then the first layer of 1mm ply deck is glued on with PVA and held down with masking tape. The edges are trimmed and sanded,

The after deck of the sub-chaser.

and as is the deck, there should be very little filling needed. The deck openings are now cut out and the top of any frames cut away. If access were required for rudders where there is not a natural opening, I would try to hide it as much as possible; on the sub-chaser, I hid the joint under the depth-charge racks. On the first deck I would make the rudder access slightly smaller to allow a lip for the deck proper to sit on. Once I am happy with the deck I apply the second 1mm ply deck. This should be smooth and level so no filling is needed, just sanding smooth and cutting out apertures. The rubbing strakes were made from 4mm x 4mm square beech sanded to a rounded triangular shape. They required careful fitting and I found this to be the most difficult part of the hull to do.

All these craft had an extra layer of planking along the waterline, extending above and below. Eight 3mm x 1mm ply strips were cut and glued on. I have used 1mm ply on all my boats and being mostly glued I find it lasts for years, with no real

deterioration. According to the photographs only the rear deck aft of the single gun platform was planked, so as it was painted I scored the planks on with a modelling knife. The forward deck showed no sign of planking so I presume it is covered with 'aeroplane fabric' and painted as the PT boats were.

The next stage was to fit an upstand around the main opening, approximately 10mm high. This provides access to the motors, shafts, battery etc. I did not cut out the opening under the single gun platform, leaving the deck as is and used it for switches and charging plugs. I was careful to keep the part I cut out of the second deck for the opening for access to the rudders as it was a neat fit.

When the original 3in gun was replaced by a 40mm Bofors they put a raised deck forward to take the new gun, between the breakwater and the front of the bridge. This again was made from ply, 2mm this time, at the same time the breakwater was also made, as it is all one assembly.

The raised forward gun platform, added when the original 3in gun carried by this class was replaced by the 40mm Bofors.

Now it was time to tackle another tricky job, namely the spurnwater. This was first cut from card to get the correct sheer and allow for the inward curve to the bow. The shape was then transferred to 2mm ply. Two were cut and checked and fitted carefully with PVA. Once dry it is surprising how strong it is, as it needs a sand-down to tidy up the edges. Draining ports, bullring and two fairleads fitted into it at the bow, and two fairleads fitted at the stern.

Once it is all sanded down the hull is laid aside and attention then turns to the superstructure and fittings. Before moving on to this part of the boat, I would like to mention the propshafts. Most of these boats had the propeller forward of the A-frame supporting it, why I do not know. They also had a perforated sleeve where the shaft enters the hull. This setup is totally different to anything I have seen before.

Superstructure and fittings

The superstructure and gun platform was made from 2mm plastic card. Again there are some variations on the superstructure and on the gun platform but some of these were later modifications. Some details and measurements I could get from the drawings, but details such as the rear gun platform support had to be obtained from photographs using a magnifying glass. The window and door apertures were first cut out and the main parts assembled, reinforcing the corners inside with right angled plastruct. The bridge deck was fitted, allowing for the camber and the edges trimmed off with very small right-angle plastruct.

On studying the photos it appears that the stanchions were the ball type on the superstructure, and on the hull they had a small loop welded on to the side. I obtained brass ball split-pin type stanchions from James Lane for the superstructure. First I used a paper punch to punch out small disks on plastic card and glued these down under the stanchions. Then the bases were soldered to the stanchions, the plastic disks drilled and the stanchions glued in. After they were set, I quickly soldered brass

The superstructure and after gun platforms. The crew are converted racing car pit crew, mechanics and deliveryman figures. The captain was originally a traffic policeman.

wire through the them so as not to melt the plastic. If required a heat sink could be used to protect the plastic.

The gun platform aft of the wheelhouse was cut from 2mm plastic card again reinforced with plastruct angles to make the whole assembly strong and robust. On studying the photographs, it appears the outer 'wings' of the platform droop down slightly and are supported by short legs on the main deck. These were soldered from brass on to a brass channel then glued under the 'wings' at the correct height. There were ball stanchions around this area as well, with the outer ones on the wings bent outwards to give more room. Again brass wire was soldered through them and fixed to the deck. This gun deck had various panels on it, which was made from plastic card, and the area round the two Oerlikons was planked. I used strips of 1mm ply for the planking.

The mast I really enjoyed making from square section brass tube, soldered together. The crosstree was from piano wire for strength, the rest from various diameters of brass wire. The steps are

staples cut in half. The radar dome was made from plastic tube and a hemispherical dome from architectural modelmakers' supplies that do a selection of sizes. The crows' nest, again from brass, and the navigation light and brackets are soldered on and wired up.

Some of the stanchions had a canvas dodger to act as a windbreak round the flying bridge and on either side of the wheelhouse. I used solar film as used to cover model aircraft for this. It is textured like cloth and I superglued it to one stanchion at the end. When dry I pulled it taught and glued the other end. When that was dry I trimmed top and bottom and sewed it around the edges then I put the heat gun on to it. It shrinks nicely to show the stanchions and handrails.

The rear gun platform was constructed in the same way. Apart from mounting an Oerlikon it was also an air intake for the engines and access to the galley. Though there is no detail on the drawing, careful examination of various photographs showed variations in the construction under the gun platform, I presume because

The 40mm Bofors gun and ammunition lockers.

some were fitted later in the boat's life and some were built with it. As I had some excellent photographs of this particular boat on completion, with some difficulty I was able to get the details from those. The railings look as though they are a welded framework rather than stanchions and wire, so they were all soldered up and fitted.

The ammunition lockers are made from 2mm plastic card, in the form of boxes. Once they are set they are sanded on a hard flat surface (a piece of glass or steel) and any filling is done sparingly with cellulose stopper. As the stopper is cellulose it eats into the plastic and while this can be an advantage for grip it has to be used sparingly. If a lot is needed another type of filler would be better. Again the lockers are rubbed down on a flat surface with water; they are then ready for detailing. This is another part of the building I like. Looking closely at the photographs I could make out the shape of the lids and locking details, the lids being held shut by a series of looped bolts. The lids were cut and recesses filed out to allow for the 'D' loops, and fitted to

the top of the locker. The 'D' loops were brass eyebolts from Artisania and glued in the sides carefully liking up the eyebolt with the filed recess in the lid. Hinges were made and the legs from plastruct access hatches companion ways. The air intake aft of the wheelhouse and the mousetraps were all constructed in the same way, taking the details from the drawing. The aft companion way has louvre doors in it.

The liferafts were made from a commercial foam rubber seal. The base of the raft is thin strips of plastic card glued into a cross-weave and fitted into the centre. The 20mm Oerlikons as supplied had RN-type gun shields. These were removed and new ones made from plastic card and brass. The mountings are the same. The Bofors gun was taken apart, retaining the mounting and trunions but the base was discarded and a new one made from plastic card. The framework for the pedals and seats is brass rod and they are fitted to a new patterned plastic card platform at the rear.

The jackstaffs were made from brass

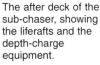

The after deck of the sub-chaser, showing the liferafts and the depth-charge equipment.

The depth charge
racks and throwers.

tube with the lights' earth wire cut short and soldered to the staff, leaving only one wire to go through the tube letting me use a thinner tube. The earth is picked up underneath the deck again. The gun guardrails were made again from brass wire and soldered together. The fire hoses are thin shoelaces dipped in emulsion paint and flattened to replicate the flattened weave of the hose.

The depth charge racks and roller racks are made from brass angle, built around a wooden block. The detail was taken from photographs, which fortunately were very clear and taken from a lot of different angles, while the dimensions were taken from the drawing. I found I could not find any flat brass which would be equivalent to flat steel bar, so I used flat stainless steel from a lorry wiper blade as some parts of the racks are constructed with flat bar. While these racks took some time to make I got a lot of satisfaction in making them, as they are a focal point of the boat. The depth charges were made from 16mm brass tube with a plastic disk glued into each end recessed about 1mm, then detailed with small plastic discs at each end to replicate the firing pistons and charge filling holes. Brass eyelets and loops were used for the lifting eyes. Electrical

insulators on the rigging were made from small sewing beads. Interior furnishings of the wheelhouse, radio etc, were taken from the drawings and made of plastic card.

The crew figures came from an assortment of sources. The captain is a traffic cop, the two other officers are deliverymen. The mechanic actually is a mechanic, while most of the others are pitcrew for racing cars, most of which have been altered to some extent.

Controls
The wiring was kept to a minimum with both Bueler motors running off one speed controller with a 7AH 12V Nicad pack amidships operating on a two-channel set. I use Battery Eliminator Circuits (BEC) in most of my boats as it simplifies things. The receiver aerial is wired to the gun rail behind the 40mm Bofors with a plug and socket, helping ensure good reception. I have stuck to Futaba for all my radio control sets as it lets everything be interchangeable. On this set-up I have over four and a half-hours sailing with life still left in the battery.

On testing some minor problems appeared. The first was water coming in through one of the propshaft bearings and oiling tube, which was cured by a touch of

SC 1055 under way.
Note the number on
her bows, applied by
painting through a
cut-out mask.

grease on the shaft and an 'O' ring on the outside of the shaft. I have found ball races let more water past than phosphor bronze bushes. The second was radio interference, but suppressing the motors solved this. The other problem was unexpected, as I had not come across it before. There was a whine from the belts and pulleys, which turned out to be the belt tension. It has to be surprisingly slack, but they do not slip. After a few trials at the pond and once these problems were ironed out, I found the sub-chaser sails very well, is very quiet and handles extremely well and has good endurance.

The 80ft Elco PT
boat model at speed.

Painting

The painting was done by hand brush, but I think an airbrush would be better at least for the upperworks and fittings. I brushed the hull with two coats of thinned household undercoat. The two coats of red oxide under the waterline, was the nearest I could find to 'copperoid'. The two coats of haze grey above the waterline were rubbed down with 800 wet and dry between coats. The deck had two undercoats and two coats of deck blue. All the fittings, superstructure etc, if properly prepared, was fine with two coats of haze grey. Matt black was used for the waterline.

The *SC 1055* number was a bit of a problem, as I could not get the numerals the right size. In the end I photocopied the numerals from the plan (*SC 1476*) and with repeatedly altering and copying I got a very good drawing. Then I gave it to a friend who makes vinyls for signs and he cut them out in mask. All I had to do was apply the mask and paint through, I was very happy with the result. I used Letraset for the draught markings.

So there it is. As a subject I thoroughly enjoyed it, and there was good availability of references. The model looks good and sails very well. All the methods I have used on the sub-chaser is applicable to other boats. I have also built an 80ft Elco using the same method and it performs very well too, in particular the geared belt drive motor. Once set up it requires little or no maintenance.

8
Large-Scale Static Display Models: USS *Enterprise* 1975

BY STEPHEN W HENNINGER

W hen I decided to build my model of the nuclear-powered aircraft carrier *Enterprise* in late 1970, all I knew was this: it would not be a collaborative effort – I would be the sole builder of the model; it would be the USS *Enterprise*, the most significant naval vessel of its day; it would be in 1:100 scale, matching an excellent Tamiya 1:100 fighter jet and helicopter series that included at least six important US naval aircraft; and it

would be a full-hull static exhibition model. I had little idea of how to proceed but had a sense that this project was what I was destined to do. Much like owning a dog, there are times in life when one must, and other times when one should not. Loyalty to the project and a determination to see it through to the end would become a solemn responsibility; in my mind abandoning it would be a serious personal failure. Thus, equipped with more will than skill, I

Nineteen years after the exhibit was dedicated at the National Air and Space Museum, model Captain Henninger applies some tender loving care to aircraft spotting on the model carrier's flight deck. Both model and Captain have aged gracefully. The model has withstood a million bumps of little noses against the clear panels and millions more flash photos. Is Captain Henninger repositioning his model Porsche 911? Henninger and the famous *Spirit of St. Louis*, shown suspended over his shoulder, are the only ones to know for sure.
MARK HENNINGER

acknowledged the mission deeply planted in my fibre. The endeavour was not compatible with many competing obligations of career and family, and there were would be consequences of personal sorrow along with triumphs of achievement. In August 1982, the saga finally ended: the model was officially presented to the National Air & Space Museum for the enjoyment by millions of visitors to Washington, D.C. As my physical and mental companion for nearly twelve years – about the average life span of a beloved dog – the *Enterprise* model

project entailed relentless sacrifice in one way or another, while enriching my life in so many ways I could never have predicted.

Research and drawings

I had no previous experience to guide me and no firm project plan. I just plunged into it. My first step was to buy a roll of cheap brown wrapping paper and draw the 11ft flight deck outline. This motivated me to ponder harder questions regarding construction methods, materials, starting point, research, skills, logistics, impact on career and family, time to completion. None of these elements was trivial. How would I tackle a piece, a process, search for the 'trick' that would drive the project forward, bit by tiny bit? I would often discover that just knowing how to make a thousand pieces well could be as rewarding as completing the thousandth piece itself. I believed that everything would work out as

Early in the model-building effort, Henninger obtained drawings such as these through a model magazine. The *Enterprise* contractor, Newport News Shipbuilding and Dry Dock, released ten such drawings. These drawings were the genesis of accurately shaping the hull of the model. Although many of the interior lines were censored out, all that counted was the shape of the hull at known locations, and positions of the decks within. No other line drawings are more important than sectional, or station lines such as these. They can be compared to modern Magnetic Resonance Imaging (MRI) for medical professionals seeking to define external and internal shapes for diagnosis. They are bread slices defining the loaf. Having only a few slices of the loaf, Henninger took six months in the shadows of the Andes of Southern Peru to fill in the missing slices, and place the slices he had exactly where they belonged.

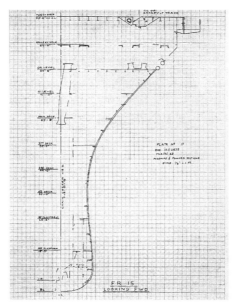

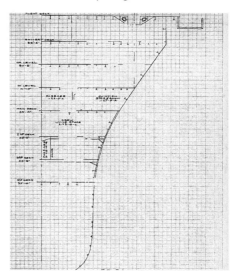

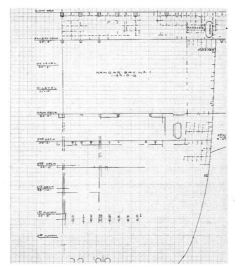

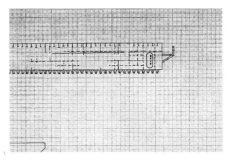

long as I kept in mind that the best ways reveal themselves through constant experimentation, and that intermittent failures define the bumpy and sometimes downright hazardous path to success.

By late 1970, the real *Enterprise* had been in service for eight years – mostly in the Western Pacific supporting the Vietnam conflict. With only several weeks to gather information before departing for a remote foreign country, I managed to obtain twelve declassified hull cross-section (station) drawings – just enough to establish fair and accurate lines for the entire length of the hull, from keel to flight deck. I also obtained profile and overhead drawings depicting earlier design concepts of the ship. These drawings, with a pedigree traceable to the shipyard, were simplified and declassified versions of the ship's evolving design process. There was no doubt as to their basic accuracy. A splendid small 1:720-scale plastic model by Revell, the first and most accurate of many plastic models of *Enterprise* to follow, was a perfect correlation tool to supplement the line drawings. Newport News Shipbuilding gave me anecdotal information, such as commissioning literature, a colour portrait, company magazines, and so forth. At a maritime bookstore in lower Manhattan, I found *Modern Ship Design* by Annapolis professor Thomas C Gillmer, whose 1970 edition included a inside front cover spread of *Enterprise* at an advanced state of construction, and an inside back cover of the ship underway at speed. The pages in between provided the scholarly material explaining the great dynamics of large modern vessel design, construction, and testing.

This was the first body of material with which I had to work as I departed for Arequipa, Peru, in early 1971 for six months' duty at a satellite tracking station in support of a NASA experiment. The timing was excellent for preparing the drawings I would use to build the model. Each of the twelve sectional drawings was re-scaled from 1:96 to 1:100. The Revell model was scribed with tiny section lines (forty-six in all) 1cm apart. I made patterns from the small model for every one of the forty-six sections, multiplied x7.2 from 1:720 to 1:100. I frequently compared and reconciled lines from the model and the twelve sectional drawings. The two information sources matched each other very closely. After three months of drawing, checking, and iterative reconciling – and yet more refinements – the result was forty-six 1:100 sectional drawings representing the ship at equal 2.83in (7.2cm) intervals from fore point to aft point, keel to flight deck. Each drawing was 'shaved' ⅟₁₆in along the hull sides and bottom using a red pen, and ³⁄₁₆in was shaved off the hangar and flight decks. The redlines thus compensated for the ⅟₁₆in birch-ply hull covering material, and the ³⁄₁₆in birch-ply flight and hangar deck coverings. This planning and drawing process consumed all of my six months in Peru. I made copies and shipped them back to New York, while I carried the originals – the Holy Grail of the project – back to the United States. My first great lesson: with accurate hull drawings, one has a ship; without them, nothing. I largely ignored details during this early phase, as they tended to be great thieves of time. Inevitably, however, the lure of some details was compelling, so I built several aircraft models of the type and scale I expected to have by the dozen, just to see what they would look like. I also built early versions of anchors, propellers, yellow tractors, and the Tilly crane. I would discover throughout the long project that the air wing construction would be an escape from the tedium of building the ship. I also had to face the reality that occasional 'down time' from the entire project was essential for overall mental health.

Starting construction

In New York during the summer of 1971, I cut all forty-six sections from ½in particleboard. I consumed about ten 4ft x 8ft sheets and wore down my father's 60-

This Polaroid photo, the only one that exists of the skeleton of CVAN-65, was taken in the basement of the model-maker's parents over thirty years ago. The pieces were all cut on his father's band saw. The back half nearest the camera was taken to South Africa; it became part of the model. The front half was put in inaccessible storage somewhere in Salisbury, MD (near Pocomoke City) and retrieved after Henninger came back from South Africa in early 1976. He still has the front half in the attic, and still uses his fathers' band saw almost every day.

year-old bandsaw and several blades in the seven-day process. Particleboard is often scoffed at by many who associate the material with cheap furniture, but it is, in fact, an economical, strong, lasting and stable resinwood product that accommodates omni-directional cutting, easy and strong bonding, sanding, machining and drilling. The material, although somewhat crumbly if not handled carefully, offered another great feature: world-wide availability. It held yet another personally important plus: in conjunction with aliphatic resin glues and aircraft-grade plywood, I eliminated most of the toxic chemical characteristics of other building techniques, particularly those associated with fibreglass. The smells and the liquid mess of glassing, regardless of the benefits, was simply not the world I wanted to get myself into – for the sake of my lungs, my family, and my close neighbours.

I test-fitted the forty-six sections at 2.83in intervals spaced along centreline alignment rods. The form of the ship was

clearly defined, spanning almost the entire 11ft and really looking like an aircraft carrier once the flight and hangar deck plywood forms were in place. I trimmed the sections to a finer continuity and taper (mostly by eye) for more accurate frame-to-plate interfacing using conventional scraping, shaping and sanding methods. I split the model effort in half and began work on the twenty-three forward sections. I mounted them upside down on a 6ft strongback with sufficient accuracy, and covered the forward hull with $\frac{1}{16}$in birch plywood. Paper patterns, cut large and small depending on the hull curvature, established the arrangement of the plywood plates. Each opposing plate was mounted alternately port and starboard to cancel a-symmetric stress buildup. Aliphatic resin glue was expected to deliver the strongest, most economical and reliable bond that would withstand the test of time in the dry, static environment of a case-protected exhibition model. I ran out of time to plate the aft section of the model, so I disassembled and packed aft hull forms for shipment to my next long-term assignment overseas.

In late summer 1971, I spent just one month on top of a cold mountain in Chile, assigned to the continuation of the same NASA experiment that sent me to Peru some months earlier. In this harsh 12,000ft-high outpost with no amenities and little electricity, I could only make notes and sketches. These early ideas were thoughtfully developed and provided a sound foundation for all that followed. Later, I would have better ideas based on more experience and better information, and various structures of the ship and aircraft would be built several times over. These first notes on the mountaintop nevertheless were among the earliest steps in the evolving process, and thus vital to the forward movement of the project.

After Chile, I accepted a longer-term assignment to a satellite tracking site near Johannesburg, South Africa. I had only several weeks in New York to round up more materials and ship them along with the aft sections to South Africa. I packed the forward hull for deep long-term storage, for I expected to be assigned to South Africa for only a year, possibly less. Once there, I built the back half of the ship in exactly the same manner as the forward half, while my assignment dragged into its second year. My stay in South Africa would be much longer, and having just the back half of a ship was now unacceptable. With the front half stored half a world away, it was unretrievable, so by mid-1973 I built the front section again, rendering the original front section surplus to requirements. Although I now had built three halves of a ship, I finally had the two halves comprising the entire model in one place.

Visiting the *Enterprise*

By 1974 my South Africa stay was into its third year. I was not only coming to the end of my information stream, but also going

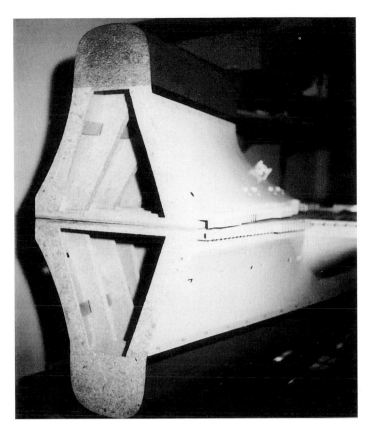

into a serious 'inspiration slump'. I had access to fine hobby stores and outlets for wood, hardware, paint, metals, plastics, photoprocessing, and copier services, but I was losing touch with the culture of my own country and with the US Navy. By now the real *Enterprise* was changing in ways that were making my early information insufficient and outdated. In the four years that had passed, I had not seen the real ship, and important details were emerging, now that the fundamental construction effort was behind me. The aircraft mix had changed. All the F-4 Phantom and A-4 Skyhawk models I had built from Tamiya kits – at least thirty in all – were now off the real ship. The F-14 Tomcat replaced the F-4, and the A-7 Corsair II had replaced the A-4 Skyhawk long ago. No models for the F-14 existed yet, and I had only a few of the A-7s. I did not really know the complete mix of aircraft on a nuclear attack aircraft carrier in late 1974, and, quite frankly, I had little or no

This Polaroid photo was taken in South Africa about 1973. This configuration was not part of the effort to cut the ship into four parts in order to send it back to the United States as described in the chapter (that happened in mid-1975), but demonstrates essentially the same concept. The bow was entered in a Johannesburg hobby show, where it and a few aircraft on the deck earned a bronze medal. Henninger's modelling skills were not yet in the gold medal category in 1973, but he treasures his South African bronze medal.

feel for the ship in all its intricate detail and operations. I simply did not fully understand what I was doing anymore. I lacked details on catwalks, external structural members, fittings, the radar suite, even basic colours, markings, and just about everything beyond the point I had reached. I was only guessing at the essence of some very important large and small details that simply could not be extracted from my limited collection of photos, and I knew I would get it all wrong if things went on this way much longer. Discouragement was setting in very fast, and by late 1974, my project eventually stalled.

I had to visit the ship very soon and see everything for myself – all modellers know when that time arrives. Then, a sudden stroke of luck: very quick and miraculous connections evolved between the *Enterprise* command structure and myself. My invitation to visit the ship came in early 1975. But there was a problem: I was in Johannesburg and *Enterprise* would be in Singapore – maybe. Those two points on the globe were extremely difficult to connect in those days. I had three days' notice, and only one flight a week from Johannesburg directly to the Orient. The airfare was among the most expensive on a per-mile basis. The movements of any warship were unpredictable – but especially so in this case, for *Enterprise* was facing the impending fall of South Vietnam, which actually happened in March and April 1975. Thin human resources at my duty station and an extra heavy workload caused friction among my colleagues. This trip would become the most stressful I ever experienced. Even if everything went perfectly, as rarely it does, only a slim chance of a successful link-up with *Enterprise* was possible. This slim window of opportunity was acknowledged grimly by the travel agent who was frantically booking my trip while I was trying just as frantically to finance it.

I decided to go. I misplaced my passport and other travel documents in Sri Lanka for a while. The connecting Boeing 707 from Frankfurt was grounded with an engine problem for several more precious hours there. Finally approaching Singapore late at night with only hours to spare, I saw the lights of *Enterprise* in the harbour directly below. I just about wanted to open the door, jump out into the dark night, and somehow land on her deck before she steamed away from me. After a restless night, I boarded her in the morning in a more conventional way. I spent six days at sea aboard *Enterprise* with her brand new pair of F-14 squadrons. I had a good SLR camera, plenty of film and the liberty to use it; I got the information and flavour of the real thing. The project was fully recharged, and so was I! Not only did the ship become real to me, but so too did the team that made it all work. No single experience would match the reward for risk of that long trip, probably not in my entire lifetime.

Shipping the model

My time in South Africa was finally approaching its end in December 1975. For over four years the model went from half a skeletal form to an 11ft fully recognisable model with a substantial but as yet incomplete array of fittings, and a partial air wing. Then, to my amazement, a small Japanese company had just introduced a 1:100-scale F-14 Tomcat model. I bought thirty. With additional A-7 Corsairs, my air wing was by now formidable. Even so, I would have to scratch-build three RA-5 Vigilantes, four E-2 Hawkeyes, and three EA-6 Prowlers. Although the EA-6 shared some common airframe with the Tamiya A-6 Intruder, the conversion would be a formidable challenge. A single C-1 'COD' was also to be built from scratch. Eleven scratch-builts would constitute about 15 per cent of the entire air wing for this exhibit.

One of the most unusual and challenging realities of leaving South Africa for return to the United States involved shipping the model in an affordable way. As a personal project without official sanction of any kind, the model had to be packaged into household-sized shipping crates within my personal shipping allowance. I could not afford the enormous surcharge of a 12ft container, nor could the shipper be responsible for such a large delicate cargo without a great insurance premium. The model therefore had to be cut into four equal sections, right through selected stations, to get it sized down to within my allowable cubic volume.

I had anticipated this issue but had hoped dismemberment of the hull might not be necessary. But it was. The particleboard sectional frames had been pre-selected; their locations were externally marked. Each of the three cut planes were carefully scribed, and a ⅛in-wide groove was cut about ¼in deep all the way around the entire ship. For each cut, I manually drove a large cross-cut saw all the way around the model and through to separation, tracking within the groove. It was an arduous process, but it worked quite well. Once all three cuts were completed, I had four equal-length sections that could be precisely rejoined in the United States – although neither easily nor quickly. Each section was almost 3ft long, almost 3ft wide (except for the much narrower bow), and 1ft high. I built four custom wood boxes and packaged each section tightly. Three additional containers housed other project elements: one for the island structure; one for all the aircraft; and one for all the research materials, kits, and building tools. They fitted within the standard containers for household effects for which I was authorised. And yes, the hollow insides of the ship sections were packed with clothing, kitchen utensils, dishes, bedding, and small appliances.

Arriving in Cambridge, Massachusetts, in January 1976 from summery South Africa with no winter wardrobe, I was never, ever, so cold in my life. My project was suspended for about eight months to tend to other matters in my life. In August

I relocated to Boulder, Colorado. I was thereafter to live and work on the project within a mobile home that was much too small for comfort. Nevertheless, I was happy to be home in America, in the legendary laid-back Boulder community, which is familiar with strange people driven by odd goals in life. That suited me just fine – at least for the next six years that it would take me to get *Enterprise* done.

Construction resumed

The two forward sections and the two aft sections of the hull were rejoined using ⅛in-thick wood spacers cut identically to the hull interfaces, replacing the material that became sawdust during the saw cuts in South Africa. The cut scars were filled, sanded, blended, and painted. The ship went from four to two equal sections once again, much as it had started out. It would remain in two sections for the next four years, mainly for convenience of movement within the tight confinement of my little workshop built on one side of the undersized mobile home. As previously mentioned, this was a project without a team, and I had to manage the model alone. I attached the two hull sections temporarily to effectively work the full hull within the confines of my tiny space. Overseeing the scope of the entire project was always essential for inspiration and visualisation. I was able to detach them anytime to move the project around for work on particular areas as needed.

The model was moved around a little but essentially stayed in one place from 1977 until August 1982. Those five and a half years were the most productive years for detailing. I had all the photos, anecdotes, advice, correspondence, and appreciation for what had become 'my ship'. The hangar deck was fitted with walls that would be viewed from the three starboard aircraft elevator openings. The hangar ceiling was installed along with simulated recessed lighting and sprinkler pipes, crane tracks, and fuel tank racks. I

The model's hanger, seen here in the late-1970s, seems cavernous but was an unfriendly place, often negotiated blindly by probing fingers and articulated elbows and wrists passing through 3in-high aircraft doors. Mirrors placed inside often helped guide tools and hardware into place. Henninger has committed to engineer a better way to access a model's inner sanctum if he ever attempted another modelling project of this scale. In his own words, 'I never let the same old way of doing things get in the way of new ideas.'

worked through all four elevator openings, the stern cavity, and the gap between the unjoined sections for all hangar deck work. With the hull sections inverted, I took advantage of gravity and weights pressing ceiling components into permanent position. No ceiling parts ever separated and drooped under the relentless pull of gravity over time, an ugly phenomenon that usually afflicts the headliner of the ageing family automobile. Perhaps I should have provided access to the hangar from the flight deck, but I thought topside access panels would spoil the flight deck no matter how I disguised the seams. In the long term, only the three starboard aircraft doors provided access to the hangar space. Replacing fluorescent lamp tubes or reaching deep into the space for any reason had become very difficult as my hands and arms thickened with age, rendering difficult or impossible doing very much inside the 3in high, 7ft long chamber. The three mini-fluorescent lamp fixtures that provided hangar lighting eventually became impossible to access, so as the lamps burned out, they stayed out. In addition, the electrical ballast for each lamp and the lamp tubes themselves generated heat

within the hull. With lamps cycling on and off at least once a day, temperature and moisture changes probably caused unwelcome stress on the model. Recognising the potential fire hazard, I eventually abandoned hangar lighting.

The Air Wing

The air wing received much attention during the final years in Colorado. With the exhibit frozen to March 1975, *Enterprise* was still designated as an attack aircraft carrier (CVAN-65, 'A' for Attack) and would be for several more months until July 1975. The aircraft mix on my model was primarily offensive. The complement included twenty-four F-14 Tomcats, twenty-four A-7 Corsair IIs, eighteen A-6 and KA-6 Intruders, three EA-6 Prowlers, three E-2 Hawkeyes, six SH-3 Sea Kings (helicopters), three RA-5 Vigilantes, and one C-1 'COD' – totalling eighty-two aircraft. I would eventually include two UH-46 Sea Knights (helicopters), and one TA-4 Skyhawk, topping out at eighty-five aircraft in all. About fifty-five were to be positioned on the flight deck or the elevators; thirty would be down below in the hangar. This was a classic representation of the ship 'loaded for bear' during the height of the Cold War.

In July 1976, *Enterprise* was redesignated CVN-65 ('Attack' designation dropped, multi-role configuration adopted). Vigilantes were removed, and S-3 Vikings came aboard for the long-range sub patrol role. My CVAN-65 exhibit would not have Vikings, nor some of the newer aircraft such as the F/A-18 Hornet, nor older aircraft such as the venerable F-4 Phantom II, A-4Skyhawk, A-3D Skywarrior or F-8 Crusader. Freezing an exhibit includes as much as it excludes, proving that not everyone can be invited to the party.

Each aircraft was authentically marked according to squadron and ship/theatre tail letters (November Kilo – NK – for *Enterprise*). I made and applied <u>all</u> of the decals, vinyl colour markings, dry transfer lettering and numbering, one by one, for every aircraft and helicopter. I estimate over 10,000 individual pieces of decoration for all the flight units. If I was

This photograph, taken about 1978 in Boulder, Colorado, shows the variety of the developing air wing. The ship, with a lot of work to go as evidenced by missing deck-edge detail, shared Henninger's time with the aircraft construction project. Never since the end of the Cold War era would American aircraft carriers have the colour, variety, and quantity of aircraft that populated the decks when their mission involved superpower rivalry. Budget, threat priorities, recruitment, social changes, etc., continue to change the nature of the deployment mission of the aircraft carrier. In 1975, however, up to twelve aircraft types might be deployed or visiting the ship for one reason or another. The E2 Hawkeyes in the foreground, A-7 Corsair IIs lined up along the runway foul line, the SH-3 Sea King helicopters nosed up to the island, the F-14 Tomcat ready for launch, and an RA-5C Vigilante waiting behind the blast deflector were all typically assigned to the ship. The UH-46 Chinook helicopters, two of which are parked between the Hawkeyes and the Corsairs, were not assigned to Enterprise but performed multiple roles that brought them aboard from time to time. The Chinooks, with a ramp entry in the rear, accommodated the captain's Porsche 911 at one time. Since 1982, Captain Henninger has hidden the car somewhere on the ship.

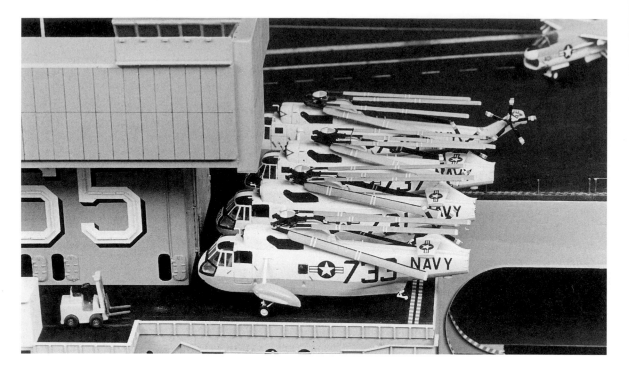

A row of SH-3 Sea King helicopters are stashed against the forward side of the model's island structure. They show how tightly aircraft can be packed within the space limits of the carrier. Everything that can be folded is folded on three of the units: rotors and tailpieces. The fourth SH-3 has its tail still extended. This set of helicopters has assumed this position for the entire nineteen years that the exhibit has been on display at the National Air & Space Museum. They are great subjects, very white and extensively decorated with large numbers, letters, and insignias. They represent one of the best plastic models ever produced, certainly in 1:100 scale.

not satisfied with my previous workmanship, I would tear down a whole set of aircraft and rebuild them to more accomplished standards. This happened often, occasionally several times over. The aircraft project probably constituted at least one-third of the entire effort. Aircraft support gear, such as tractors, starting units, fire vehicles, the Tilly crane, and tow bars, comprised scores of additional scratch-built pieces.

The 1975-era model retained the original distinctive look of the unique beehive cap of the island structure, which was not changed until about 1980. With a few exceptions, I largely prefer the original appearance of ships, because the designers' idealism is reflected in its architecture. Later changes usually are forced by practical realities, which hardly ever improve the aesthetics of any ship.

Final completion

My model made its way into the Smithsonian National Air & Space Museum for several reasons. First, I loved the museum ever since it opened July 1976;

it was the only place I would donate the ship if it was accepted for prominent display. Second, the museum had no aircraft carrier model as of 1981 and certainly needed one. Third, it boiled down to simple luck and timing, which is always unexplainable. On impulse, I asked to see the aeronautics curator, and showed him photos of the model. He agreed to meet with the museum director, who said: 'Let's get it.' In early 1982, the director visited my tiny Boulder mobile home, saw the ship in the little workshop and immediately asked: 'Can we have it by summer [1982]?' 'Yes,' I said, thereby committing myself to almost interminable hours to wrap up the final details.

The final push was underway. Catwalks, some built eleven years before from 0.5mm plywood and aluminium, were permanently mounted around the entire flight deck – over 22 linear feet. I completed life baskets containing mass abandonment survival gear, at least 100 of them, each comprising about forty soldered wire pieces. I mounted them in place outboard of the catwalks. Hose reels for multiple fuelling stations were all handmade

and installed. Inclined companionways, open hatches, life rails, life nets, and structural beams of many forms further defined the complex world of the flight deck edge. The four engagement wires, and runout apparatus contributed to the important story of aircraft arrestment. Catapult tracks, blast deflectors, and ordinance elevators were completed. Thousands of deck tiedown circles – made from teletype chad – were placed in an overall diamond grid pattern as accurately as possible on all aircraft service decks. Red/yellow striped safety lines surrounded high risk areas. 'BEWARE OF JET BLAST, PROPS, AND ROTORS' signs on the island were handmade. The Fresnel Mirror Landing System was a moderately difficult subassembly project, crucial to the exhibit for the many naval aviators who would view the model. While all this building was going on during the final push to the finish, the Navy granted me another week's stay aboard the ship, and I was thus able to 'inhale more jet fuel' for inspiration.

At one point, however, the model came extremely close to destruction, along with my entire home. One mid-winter night, the violent jet stream dipped down into the Rocky Mountains and funnelled directly into Boulder. These 'Chinook' winds, heated by compression and friction, severely damaged parts of the city. My mobile home came very close to collapsing under the hammering force of record-breaking 130mph gusts. Severed gas lines threatened to blow up structures around my home. I fought back by building makeshift wall buttresses, and even held onto doors and windows that seemed to be failing. At the nearby airport, small planes were ripped from their moorings and slammed against hangars. Street signs sliced their way into light poles and through picture windows. Roof debris was everywhere. Just barely in time before my home reached the limit of its endurance, the winds snaked back up into the stratosphere. After six hours of this climatological mayhem, the event ended, and the model had just barely survived.

In July 1982, the model was permanently joined amidships into one complete hull. This was a risky and time-consuming job, because by then almost everything on the model was finished.

The E-2 Hawkeye was one of the four most complicated of the scratch-built aircraft in the air wing's inventory. Four were built, with only this one spread-winged. Three folded-winged units are on the flight deck or on the elevator. Since they are considered valuable contributions to the exhibit, they are not hidden inside the hangar. The spread-winged unit began its career as a 'show-off' piece on the bow catapult, about to be launched. When the exhibit was reconfigured to open up the runway area for recovery, it was selected to be the 'airborne' piece. Since 1991, it has been mounted on its tailhook, frozen in flight, just about to catch the #3 wire, where it is located on the exhibit today.

The Smithsonian Institution invited all nine *Enterprise* Captains, including the then-current commanding officer, to the model's debut; three came. Also in attendance at the dedication of this one-of-a-kind carrier exhibit was the president of Newport News Shipbuilding, the National Air and Space Museum director and curator, friends, and family. After coffee and cake, the stanchions were moved aside, and the public swarmed in.

Doing a major structural job at that point easily could have set back the project if one false move, or chemical eruption blending wrong paints, or any number of awful scenarios had played out. Everything worked out, however, and finally the ship was over 11ft long once again. It was much too heavy and cumbersome for movement by one person. I had pre-positioned the model to easily slip out of the workshop with the aid of four people, to be placed in a box I had built for this one important journey. I was able to walk around the entire ship during the final weeks and tend to the small things that always needed adding, upgrading, and enhancing. A strange panic swept over me in these last weeks, because I realised that detailing a nuclear aircraft carrier could consume several lifetimes. Finishing this project was simply a 'declaration' more than anything

else, for the true goal of completion would always be within sight buy never within grasp. In August 1982, the model was therefore 'declared' finished, boxed and loaded aboard a rental truck for the 1950-mile journey to Washington, D.C. The Smithsonian constructed a viewer-friendly walkaround exhibit case with overhead lighting and a low base for child viewing (inspiring children was very important to me). A woodworking friend built a walnut base with several hundred blocks replicating a drydock. I considered this presentation the best way to represent the size and mass of such a great naval ship – much more impressive than brassy pedestal mounts for this special purpose, particularly for children who often see the exhibit from an underside perspective.

On 20 August 1982, the model was dedicated at the Air & Space Museum, in ceremonies attended by three former *Enterprise* commanding officers, members and guests of my family, Newport News Shipyard officials, and Smithsonian staff. It has been on continuous display ever since that day. Its recent and temporary neighbour, Charles Lindbergh's *Spirit of St. Louis*, honoured my labour of love by spanning its left wing over the model. Never could I imagine that such history would surround this exhibit, this very part of me. From the humble beginnings of an idea in a parking lot almost twelve years before, spurred on by the dare of a colleague, the model came into being by sheer force of will, and perhaps a dash of foolishness.

The model enjoys many visitors at the museum, but some things about the exhibit are quirky. For example, my car was a beloved white 1968 Porsche 911. Its 1:100-scale likeness hides in partial view somewhere on the *Enterprise* model at all times. When I clean, alter, and tidy up the exhibit every couple of years, the location of the little white sports car is changed. It has become something of a Washington legacy. Many who see the model try to find 'the Captains' Porsche'.

The Acting Director of the National Air and Space Museum

cordially invites you to attend

a coffee marking the installation of

a model of the U.S.S. ENTERPRISE

Friday morning, August the twentieth

Eight-thirty o'clock

Sea-Air Operations gallery
National Air and Space Museum
Independence Avenue and Sixth Street, S.W.
Washington City

RSVP (202) 357-1663   *Invitation admits one*
                                         Non transferable

The *Enterprise* model rests on several hundred walnut-capped blocks simulating a drydock. The plaque provides a history of the ship with specifications, as well as a timeline describing the milestones of building the model itself. MARK HENNINGER

On 20 August 1982, the Smithsonian Institution's National Air and Space Museum welcomed the unique 12ft mode of the USS *Enterprise* CVAN 65 with a dedication ceremony. The Enterprise model's captain and creator, Steve Henninger (far left) stands with the real carrier's seventh, fifth, and second commanding officers. On Henninger's left are Carol C Smith, Forrest S Petersen, and Frederick H Michalis. With all three naval officers now deceased, this special photo preserves fond memories for Henninger and reminds him of the high level of respect he received from these Navy leaders.

During the installation process, each of the two pairs of five-bladed propellers was placed on the wrong side of the ship. I tried to correct the problem immediately, but one prop was stuck on its shaft, so none of the others could be relocated without the risk of breakage. I left the problem as it was, and I wondered how many viewers would call the museum or me on this error. Marine professionals know that all ships with multi-screw arrangements have the 'wheels' spinning topside outwards: port set counter-clockwise, starboard set clockwise. When I finally was able to prepare four genuine bronze replacement props in 1986, the propulsion gear was overhauled and the original stubborn propeller was forcefully removed along with the other three originals. The new bronze pieces were placed on the correct shafts. I never was called on the error.

I am so grateful for all the visitors who have taken the time, from moments to hours, to view and sometimes study my 1:100-scale *Enterprise*. No doubt, some look at a model, and others see the ship. To all interested viewers, thank you for your praises and your critiques. I am flattered that my model has inspired the birth of other *Enterprise* models. And although I have heard about models built better and more complete, I hope mine remains the old top dog awhile longer. After all, this model was not only a destination, but also a journey of passion and passage.

9
Radio-Controlled Model Submarines: USS *Skipjack* 1959

BY DAVID MERRIMAN III

The hobby of radio-controlled (R/C) vehicles holds a special fascination for a unique group of model builders. We are the type who enjoy the interactive manipulation of devices of our own creation, building and operating miniature models that replicate the look and function of a real-life prototype. As a young man I served aboard both conventional (diesel/electric) and nuclear powered submarines. Today, I am a professional model builder and an R/C model hobbyist. Not too surprising, then, that I turned to designing, building, and operating R/C submarine models in my later years.

R/C submarining is a relatively new

The completed 1:96 scale R/C model of a *Skipjack* class submarine.

aspect of the hobby, and I suggest for those of you interested in learning more about this activity to join an international organisation that supports this hobby. The SubCommittee prints a quarterly magazine and organises R/C submarine activities throughout the world. Additional recommended reading includes *Simply Submarines*, and *Model Submarine Technology*, both published by Traplet Publications. Looking back, it would have been useful, when I began in this hobby, to have had such resources available to me – I would not have had such a steep learning curve to climb.

The current availability of reliable, small, lightweight, and highly capable R/C systems gives the advanced model builder the ability to animate just about any model vehicle he wishes. But, the advances within the craft have only occurred through the determined efforts of the innovators within the field. For example, the building of R/C model helicopters was once considered only the purview of master mechanics and aerospace engineers, but now through the perfection and distribution of reliable R/C helicopter rotor heads, transmissions, and stabilisation devices, almost anyone with the money, time, and reflexes can enjoy the hobby of R/C helicopter operation. R/C submarine operation is experiencing a similar growth cycle. Outfits like SubTech, OTW, Engel, and other speciality equipment manufacturers have done the experimentation and the engineering, and are catering to the demands of this growing market, actively advancing the hobby. Today, with commercially available watertight containers, specialised artificial stability devices, and easy to assemble submarine hull kits, the hobby continues to expand, taking its legitimate place on the scene. R/C submarines are a reality. It is my intention here to entice you to consider joining the 'bubble-head' ranks as I introduce you to the process I employed to design, build and operate my 1:96 scale *Skipjack* submarine model.

So, How Does an R/C Submarine Model Work?

Like other types of R/C models it is easier to understand the means of locomotion and control of the vehicle if we drop the word 'model'. Miniature vehicles operate in the same manner and travel through the same environment as their full-scale prototype. R/C submarines are in every sense practical little vessels, not toys.

A model submarine has to perform the same tasks as the 'real thing': it has to propel itself through the water, change its displacement in order to cruise above or beneath the surface with ease, and have the means to keep the water away from the electronic and mechanical devices that have to remain dry.

Buoyancy and the need to change the submarine's weight

There are model submarines that dive underwater through brute force. These speed through the water with horizontal control surfaces deflected to force the hull to 'dynamically' dive the boat under against the excessive drag forces presented by their buoyant hulls, but they operate in a most unrealistic manner. Proper R/C submarines change their weight to account for the displacement change that occurs as the boat completely immerses itself beneath the surface.

Those builders who wish their R/C submarine to operate in this manner need to outfit the boat with a proper ballast tank. The quantity of water the ballast tank contains is sized to equal the weight needed to cancel the buoyant force exerted by those additional portions of the hull immersed (the structure above the waterline) when the submarine is fully dived. Regardless of how a ballast system gets the water in and out of the ballast tank, the effect is the same. Pumps, pistons, collapsible bags, compressors – all of these are effective means of moving the water in and out of the tanks. Each method has its virtues and liabilities. The one I favour, for its simplicity and ease of maintenance, is the

'gas' type, where the ballast tank is open to the water at the bottom. When dry, the air (or other gas) within the ballast tank is nearly equal to the ambient water pressure, regardless of depth. Therefore, the gas-type ballast tank can be a lightweight, simple structure. To flood the ballast tank a valve atop it is opened, permitting the trapped gas to vent off as water rushes in through the opening(s) in the bottom to fill it. With the ballast tank full of water, the weight of the water taken on negates the upward buoyant force exerted by those structures normally above water. The submarine sinks. It assumes a state of equilibrium and is said to be 'neutrally buoyant'.

The dynamics of the submerged submarine
Both water and air are fluids, and other than water's near inability to be compressed (a characteristic only of interest to those operating high-performance vehicles) there are many parallels between the effects they have on bodies moving through them (many submarine dynamic study models

are actually tested in wind tunnels). Water, like air, offers resistance to a body in motion through it. This friction, more commonly expressed as 'drag', has to be overcome through the production of thrust.

A submarine achieves motion through its fluid by acting on it with a propeller, a device that accelerates a quantity of the fluid in one direction, the reaction against that fluid producing a thrusting force that propels the vehicle in the other direction. For a given speed through a fluid a submarine's propeller produces an amount of thrust equal to the drag the fluid imparts on the submarine.

As a vehicle, like a submarine or aircraft, travels through the fluid it can act on the fluid with the aid of 'control surfaces' to change its orientation to the flow of the fluid around it. The 'angle of attack' of the vehicle's hull and/or wings to its direction of motion through the fluid creates 'lift'; change the angle of attack in the yaw plane and the hull 'lifts' to the left

A practical 'wet hull' type R/C submarine must allow water to enter/exit the hull quickly – the only dry element is the WTC contained within the free-flooding hull. Taking advantage of the deeply engraved outlines representing the many flood/drain points on the bottom hull I worked with drill, file, and sandpaper to open these areas up to admit water.

or right; change the angle of attack in the pitch plane, and the hull 'lifts' up or down. And just as an aircraft, a submerged submarine uses its vertical and horizontal control surfaces to change its angle of attack to the fluid flow, thus effecting a turn or diving/rising.

Keeping the water out

There are many parallels between a submarine and an aircraft operating within their respective fluids. However, a model submarine additionally needs to keep the water out of spaces that must remain dry. A strong pressure hull has to be provided to contain the motor, the circuitry and the mechanics that propel and control the submarine. Special watertight seals have to girdle the propulsion drive shaft(s) and control surface/device-actuating push rods.

There are two schools of thought on how best to achieve this watertight requirement. One favours a 'dry hull', making the entire structure of the submarine (or a substantial portion of it) the watertight envelope. The advantage with this is that the entire hull presents itself for equipment storage, and it becomes a relatively easy matter to place and maintain the operating systems aboard. However, since 'dry hull' R/C submarines present such a high displacement, a great deal of fixed weight has to be installed to make the model heavy enough to float at the designed waterline. Incorporating all the watertight seals in hard-to-reach portions of the hull is a drawback of 'dry hull' model submarines. Typically the ballast tank of these models has to be large, as most of the above-waterline portions of structure displace so much more water when immersed as compared to a 'wet hull' type, resulting in a very heavy model which can be difficult to transport.

The 'wet hull' R/C submarine, the type I favour and discuss in some detail in this chapter, is generally easier to maintain and transport. Basically, the hull and other structures are free flooding. A separate internal water/pressure proof watertight

cylinder (WTC), within the hull, houses those items that need to operate dry.

Virtues and liabilities of the Skipjack design

I chose 1:96 scale for my model *Skipjack*. This would produce a relatively small model, at 31in in length qualifying as carry-on baggage for air travel. Furthermore, its short turning radius would permit manoeuvring even in the smallest of swimming pools. My *Skipjack* submarine is a dead-on scale model, *ie* there is no enlargement of control surfaces or other departures from the geometry of the prototype. Therefore my model, unsurprisingly, demonstrates the same good and bad handling characteristics encountered by the 'real' boats.

For example, the tall sail of the *Skipjack* class induces a 'foil roll' inboard of an underwater turn, the amount of roll being a function of speed and rudder angle applied. Unfortunately, at a critical turning rate and speed the model will roll so far over that even maximum 'up' planes is not enough to counter the 'down' plane effect of the rotated rudders. An uncontrollable dive results!

However, on the positive side, my *Skipjack* model, like the prototype, has a relatively high power density, an efficient five-bladed propeller, near perfect 'teardrop' hull, and well streamlined appendages. This model goes like a bat out of hell when the throttle is firewalled! No submarine model at the lake is faster than one of my little 1:96 *Skipjack*s. But it is a handful to drive underwater and requires its operator's full, undivided attention - not a model for the faint of heart!

The *Skipjack* Class Submarine: A Historical Overview

A study of the development of the *Skipjack* class submarines follows.

The first practical military submarines appeared at the beginning of the last century. These small, unreliable, and barely seaworthy craft were compelled to spend most of their time on the surface as their conventional main engines required massive amounts of air in order to operate. For underwater running, with few exceptions these boats made use of electric motors, drawing on massive lead-acid batteries to run for short periods of time underwater at very slow speed.

These conventional submarines (the diesel engine/electric motor combination having become the world standard between the wars) could run at a relatively high speed on the surface, permitting them to race to an attack position. Only then would the boat submerge to press the attack. This basic mode of operation dictated the design of these boats for decades, with ship-like hulls optimised for surface performance. As long as submarines were dependent on the surface to supply air for their engines, the submarine hull could not mature to the spindle form, the shape best suited to reduce submerged drag.

Two things happened after the Second World War to allow the submarine to mature to the ideal submerged hull form: the need for the submarine to counter other submarines in their true element was one, and the other was the development of nuclear power, freeing submarines from dependence on the surface forever. America took the lead by necessity. With the advent of the Cold War and the alarmingly rapid build-up of the Soviet submarine force, the mission of the American submarine became not only one of commerce raiding, but also anti-submarine warfare (ASW). US Navy submarines would have to be optimised for underwater speed, manoeuvrability, stealth and improved means of sonar location, classification, and tracking of enemy submarines.

Well into the Cold War years the American Navy's work with nuclear power had advanced through the *Nautilus*, the *Seawolf*, and the first class of attack submarines, the *Skates*. Though these revolutionary submarines were nuclear powered, all were of rather conservative hull form, optimised for efficient surface running, not underwater speed or manoeuvrability.

The 'perfect' hull form
By the late 1950s, with information in

The 'perfect' teardrop hull of the *Skipjack* class, optimised for underwater performance.

hand from studies conducted by the conventionally powered research submarine, *Albacore* (possessing a proper teardrop-shaped hull, powerful motors and exceptionally high-capacity batteries), time had come to wed the '*Albacore* hull' to the power of the unleashed atom. (Surprisingly, when one starts to research the genesis of submarine design, it is found that the so-called 'teardrop hull' is not the child of the twentieth century, but originated with the early submarine inventors like John Holland, Simon Lake, Gustave Zede, M. Goubet and others, in the mid-nineteenth century, and before, had hit on the tapered spindle form as the best possible shape for a vehicle travelling completely submerged.)

A new type of submarine to fit a new mission
The post-war submarine designs evidenced better streamlining as their ship-type hulls were finessed to lower underwater drag. However, these were interim measures only. It was not until the US Navy had logged enough hours with the first conventionally-formed nuclear boats that confidence was high enough to warrant the next step: the integration of the teardrop hull with the nuclear power plant. The first boats to see this amazing melding of technologies were the submarines of the *Skipjack* class.

The only significant departure the *Skipjack*'s designers made from underwater streamlining was the tall sail, needed to house the many sensor masts/antennas and periscopes. The height of the sail was needed to get the periscope lenses and antennas as high as possible to maximise the range of optical observation and radio/ECM/ESM reception. Keep in mind that these boats were built at a time when electronics had not advanced to the point where many different antenna functions could be integrated into a single antenna system – the sails of the *Skipjack* and her sisters contained no less than nine retractable masts and periscopes!

The tall *Skipjack* sail, specifically the dynamic loads it produced during underwater turns, accounted for the reason these boats were restricted in their ability to make high-speed underwater turns – a characteristic mimicked by my model *Skipjack*.

First the Masters, then the Tools, finally the Model Parts

Model submarine hulls have been built from a variety of materials over the years: turned and beaten metal sheet, hollowed-out wooden block, plank-on-frame wood build-up, bread-and-butter wood laminate, vacuformed plastic, machined metal, plastic pipe, even waterproofed paper, but the material of choice today is glass-reinforced plastic (GRP).

GRP describes a rather broad class of material. Basically, the term is accepted to describe a structure formed from glass fibre reinforcement impregnated with liquid resin which is then made to change state from liquid to a solid, the encapsulated glass fibres producing the strength, the plastic component fixing the form of the glass/resin material. There are several choices as to the chemistry of the saturating resin used. Polyester resin was one of the first available to the general public. It is cheap and cures to a hardness that makes for a very tough and stiff GRP structure, but it shrinks a great deal as it changes state from liquid to solid, making parts containing it subject to warping.

The hobby trades (and many advanced scratch-builders, such as myself) are, by and large, today using epoxy resin as the stiffening agent for our GRP structures. I employ the epoxy/glass system and use the marine resins produced by Gougeon Brothers. Their West System laminating epoxy is easy to use and the hardening agent of this two-part system is available in either a 'fast' or 'slow' cure version, permitting the builder to work with either large or small batches of resin at a time.

When I first sat down and began designing a 1:96 *Skipjack* R/C model submarine I had no doubt that the principle structure would be GRP. With that material I could achieve a thin, hollow hull possessing more than adequate strength and rigidity. For the non-structural elements of the model – such as the sail, tail section, control surfaces, and masts – I elected to fabricate them from hollow and solid cast polyurethane resin. The propeller and small detail items would be cast from white metal.

Research

Securing reliable drawings of modern American submarines is a very difficult task for the average guy. However, I possess an advantage in this area that most people do not enjoy. Some thirty years ago I served a tour with the staff at the Submarine Force Library and Museum (today known as The Nautilus Museum) at the time located on the Submarine Base, Groton Connecticut. I've maintained my relationship with the museum through the years. Ten years ago, while I was at the Nautilus Museum, conducting other business, the Director informed me of the availability of a recently declassified set of Ships General Plans of the Skipjack class. I was floored! Talk about serendipity!

I had been on the lookout for documentation of the design to support creation of a R/C model submarine kit I hoped to produce and market to the hobby trade. And documentation just does not get any more credible than securing a set of plans generated by the Navy's central office of ships structures and systems, the Bureau Of Ships (BuShips, later re-titled Naval Sea Systems Command).

The wooden masters

With a copy of the BuShips *Skipjack* external arrangement plans in hand I made copies and promptly sent a set off to Greg Sharpe. His outfit, Deep Sea Designs, produces and sells the finest 'model builder' plan sets of modern submarines available today. Later, having got a set of Greg's 1:96 scale drawings of *Skipjack* in hand, I commissioned Steven Reichmuth to build me a set of wooden masters. Steve is a well-known static and R/C submarine model builder who accepts the occasional commission. Steve turned a split piece of

I commissioned Steve Reichmuth, one of America's best model submarine makers, to produce the wooden masters of the *Skipjack*s. His basic shapes - an upper and lower hull half, sail, and control surfaces - were used to make intermediate GRP tools. Here we see Steve's sail master ready to be inserted into a parting board, needed to mask off half the masters form to facilitate creation of the first half of the two-part sail intermediate tool.

From the tools I produced GRP production masters which were scribed and detailed out. From those production masters I produced rubber and rubber/hard-shell production tools.

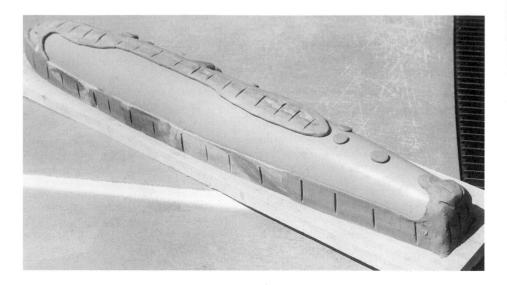

Pattern Maker's wood on his lathe, forming a two-piece master of the *Skipjack* hull. And he hand-carved a solid sail, rudders, a stern plane, and one horizontal stabiliser from wood. It was my job to convert these finished wooden pieces into GRP and resin model parts – a long and sometimes complicated process.

Unfortunately, wood is not a suitable substrate in which to scribe the many engraved lines needed to represent the access hatches, door, vents, cleats, and other items that penetrate the surface of the *Skipjack*'s hull and sail. Steve's wooden

masters could not be used directly to produce the production tools from which the model parts would be fabricated. Instead, they would be used to make 'intermediate tools', from which I would lay-up GRP 'production masters', as GRP is a material more suitable to the detailing work.

The intermediate tools

Pictured on p.119 we see my use of Steve's wooden master of the *Skipjack*'s sail to produce an intermediate tool. First, a 'parting board', a base in which a cut-out

Here we see the various control surfaces and stabilizers set half-way in backing clay and the sail and stern section set into their respective parting boards. A two-piece rubber tool will be made over the control surface masters. The sail and stern section will be used to make glove/mother mould tools will be created for the appendages, and hard-shell tools for the sail.

within it accepts half of the sail master. This presents only one-half of the master above the board's surface, positioning the sail master for fabrication of the first half of the two-part intermediate tool. Secured with clay within the parting board, the exposed surfaces of the sail and parting board surface (flange) were coated with a mould release system - layers of wax and polyvinyl alcohol (PVA). The old release produces a stick-free barrier between the tooling resin and the wooden sail master/parting board.

After laying down three laminates of epoxy/7oz fibreglass cloth, this GRP intermediate tool-half was popped off the work. The sail master was then pulled out of its parting board and reinserted into the GRP half-tool, the flanged surface of the tool and the exposed surface of the wooden sail master treated with the wax/PVA mould release barrier, and the second GRP intermediate tool half created.

After the second half-tool had cured hard, it was pulled away from the first half. The wooden sail master was then removed and put into safe storage (you never know when an original might be needed again). The two halves were given the mould release treatment within their cavities, and over their flanged faces, preparing them for lay-up of the sail production master. The same process of intermediate tool fabrication was employed to make the hull production masters.

Steve's wooden control surfaces and horizontal stabiliser masters were used to form room temperature vulcanising (RTV) silicon rubber tools. Those two-piece tools, in turn, were used to fabricate the required number of solid cast epoxy resin production masters.

The production masters

Within the hard-shell GRP sail and hull intermediate tools I first brushed in a thick mix of gel-coat, a mixture of catalysed resin (in this case, epoxy), a thickening agent (micro-balloons, talc, cotton fibres are some examples), and a colouring agent. This gel-coat produces an opaque, hard surface that is easy to scribe. Since this gel-coat is the first layer applied to the tool, it becomes the surface, or substrate, of the completed GRP production masters.

The goal is to produce GRP production masters with a surface receptive to the scribing and detail work needed to bring them to the point where they embody all the detailing observed on the prototype. This is where Greg Sharp's detailed 1:96 plans became most useful. Using the plans and photos of the real boats gathered from the museum and other sources, I set about the task of lofting the location and geometry of each engraved line onto the masters with pen and pencil. Then, with the aid of a straight edge, and both special and commercially available stencils, I carefully cut into the surface of each master, with a scribe, the engraved lines, squares, circles, and ovals needed to represent the detailing.

The production tools

With scribing completed, the production masters were prepared for creation of the production tooling. First, the two sail halves were bonded together into a single hollow unit. This production master was used to form a three-piece rubber production tool (featuring a 'core' element to make the resulting cast resin piece hollow) from which 'kit' sail parts would later be cast.

A portion at the stern of the upper and lower hull production masters was sawed off, assembled as a separate master and joined with the two cast epoxy resin horizontal stabilisers (which act as supports for the stern plane control surfaces), and this assembly used as a production master from which a three-piece rubber production tool was created. The lower hull production master was further cut into two more pieces. Later, the production hull parts could be easily assembled into a structure possessing a natural break through which the hull is accessed to install and maintain the devices needed to make the model a fully-capable R/C submarine.

The final 'production' tools needed to create the GRP *Skipjack* hull parts. These tools combine both rubber and hard-shell elements, the flexible rubber portion of these tools are located to capture the deep engraved work (in positive) from the masters, something not achievable with the stiff polyurethane tooling plastic used for the hard elements of the tool. Note the 'displacing plug' held over a formed GRP model part.

Unlike the simple wooden masters, it would not be an easy matter to make the production tools off of the deeply scribed sail, hull and stern section production masters, as those tools would have to posses the ability to tolerate the stresses imposed by the narrow engraved lines on the surface of the masters. When separated, the material of the tool had to resist the shearing forces that would otherwise break away the raised lines captured off the masters. To address this engineering challenge I devised production tools that would 'flex' free, without damage, as the closely keyed engraved lines and raised lines between master and tool (and later, tool and part) were separated. Of course, the all-rubber, multi-piece tools for the sail, control surfaces, and stern section presented no problem as they naturally flex during extraction, preventing such damage.

The big production tools for the three hull pieces on the other hand presented a problem: using rubber alone to create those tools would have been prohibitively expensive. And to use inflexible GRP hard-shell type tools to produce the deeply engraved GRP kit parts would have resulted in damage to both the production master and tools as they were separated. The solution was to make hull production tools comprised of solid elements for those portions of the master's surface devoid of engraved detail, and to incorporate into the tool RTV rubber to those areas rich in engraved detailing, producing a set of hybrid hull production tools. (I would be remiss here if I did not gratefully acknowledge the assistance of Matt Thor, a good friend, who put me onto this method of tool making.)

The hull production masters were prepared by mounting each unit on a mouldboard and covering their engraved areas with a half-inch thick layer of clay. A mould release barrier was applied, and the hard-shell element of each tool was laid-up using a special two-part filled polyurethane tool making resin available from the Freeman Company (an excellent source of specialised modelling tools, substrates, and tooling and production resins). Once the hard-shell element of the tool had hardened, it was pulled off the mouldboard, the hull master removed, and the clay scooped out. Large holes drilled into the cavities formed over the clay would later route RTV rubber into those voids. With each of the hull tools, its master was re-inserted, and the tool bolted back down onto the mouldboard. Rubber was mixed and then poured into the voids of the tools formed over the engraved portions of the master.

Once the rubber cured hard, the completed hybrid production tool was removed from the mouldboard. Then, the production master was popped out, revealing a perfectly captured tool cavity - a negative of the exact hull master shape; the simple, low draft, surfaces of the tool captured in hard tooling plastic, the deep draft detailed engraved lines captured in rubber.

As each hull production master was pulled from its tool, the slight undercuts and deep draft of the engraved work only caused the rubber within the tool to displace a little, and it sprang back into its correct position once the master cleared the tool. It is the flexibility of the rubber elements of these type hybrid tools that permits the incorporation of such deep detailing to the production parts.

Now, it would be normal practice to simply use the hybrid hull tools to give form to the production parts through the hand lay-up process. But that method is time-consuming and does not provide a means by which the interior of the thin-walled GRP structures can be rendered to a specific form. I had established a production goal of devising a means of rendering GRP kit parts with inboard structures (radial WTC foundations, for example), formed during a single-step GRP part fabrication process; a method of achieving GRP parts possessing rich surface detail, inside and out, and to do so in one operation. That goal has been achieved!

After many months of missteps, experimentation, consultation with other model builders, and a little luck, I have settled on the process described here. Pursuant to the dual goals of speeding the production process and to render hull parts with specific inner and outer surfaces, I hit upon the 'displacing plug' process.

The plug, an element of the production tool, acts to force the introduced mix of reinforcement glass and catalysed resin up against the concave surface of the tool. As the surface of the plug itself possesses specific form, the GRP part produced captures not only the tool's cavity detailing, but also the shapes imparted onto it by the plug – for example, WTC foundations, within the lower hull piece.

Laying up the GRP parts
Fabrication of the GRP parts was easy – coming up with the hybrid tools was the difficult bit! Displacing plug tooling permits single-step part fabrication that produces flawless GRP parts of specific cross section and possessing defined shape inside and out.

To make a hull GRP part, the tool cavities and displacing plug are prepared with a spray coating of a silicon-based mould release agent. A pre-determined amount of catalysed epoxy resin is mixed, some gray pigment added, and the mix poured directly into the tool cavity. A pre-cut sheet of 10oz fibreglass mat is placed into the cavity and pressed into the resin. The glass is worked into the resin with disposable brush. A serrated roller is then used to further work the resin into the fibres, which continues until the lower portion of the cavity becomes a mushy mass of resin-saturated glass fibre.

At that point I push the tool's displacing plug down into the cavity and slowly tighten its fasteners until it bottomed-out on its foundations (the height of the foundation shims set to fix a specific annular stand-off distance between the tool cavity and the plug surface). The plug is jacked down slowly to give the bigger air bubbles trapped within the resin/glass mix an opportunity to rise and escape to atmosphere. Of course, after the plug is positioned all the way down into the resin/glass mix, some air bubbles will be captured and will not escape through the very narrow space between cavity and plug before the resin solidifies. To crush the entrapped bubbles, while the resin is still liquid, the entire tool is placed into a pressure pot and subjected to a pressure of two atmospheres. The increased pressure reduces the size of the entrapped bubbles and 'crushes' them into the resin solution. The tool is left in the pot till the part cures hard (with the West System epoxy laminating resin I use, about six hours). The tool is pulled out of the pot, the mechanical fasteners that hold the tool elements together removed, the plug pulled free, and the GRP part extracted from the cavity portion of the tool. What is revealed is a gray epoxy/glassfibre part with no air-bubbles, precise wall thickness, and perfect form, inside and out – GRP model parts rendered in just one production step, not by multiply hand lay-ups!

Casting the metal and resin parts
Two- and three-piece rubber production tools were used to cast the control surfaces, stern section, sail, mast fairings, and anchor from polyurethane production resin. Cut within each tool was a single sprue hole through which the catalysed resin was introduced. Arrayed at the high points of each tool's cavities are sliced-out vent channels to permit the rapid escape of air as the liquid resin is poured in through the sprue/gate network cut into the bottom of each cavity. As with the plug GRP tools, I pressurise the freshly-introduced catalysed resin to assure bubble-free production parts. A rubber 'disc' type tool was made to render the small and delicate cast white metal parts (retractable type cleats, antennas, periscope heads, running lights, etc).

The same rubber I use for resin and GRP tool fabrication is used here. The BJB tool-making rubber I use exclusively – the end result a solid resin-casting tool, an element of a hybrid tool, or a disc-type tool

needed for centrifugal casting of low-melt metal parts – is their TC-5050 Silicon based room temperature vulcanising rubber. The cured TC-5050 has the chemical stability to withstand up to eighty polyurethane resin casting cycles, better than 200 epoxy resin casting cycles, and (so far) an unlimited number of white-metal (97 per cent tin, 3 per cent antimony alloy) casting cycles. The TC-5050 is designed to take a sustained 600° heat, which is a bit above the working temperature of molten white metal and lead. With that slight margin, the BJB tooling rubber I use is ideal for metal casting as well as the more traditional resin and GRP casting chores.

The metal casting disc tool differs in form from resin-casting tools in that its sprue hole (through which the molten metal is introduced) is located in the centre of the two-piece disc-shaped tool. The two tool halves are arranged layer-cake style with the sprue hole centred in the upper half of the tool. Mounted on a turntable, the disc tool is secured in place and set to spin about the axis of the sprue. Optimum rotational speed for casting metal parts from a particular tool is driven by the following variables: cross-section of the gates leading from the sprue, distance of the cavities from the tools centre of rotation, tool operating temperature, cavity geometry, etc.

To cast metal parts the tool is brought up to speed and molten white metal poured into the sprue hole where centrifugal force, in an instant, acts to drive the liquid metal from the sprue, through a radiating array of gate channels and into the cavities forming the part, where the metal quickly cools and sets. The tool is then stopped from rotating, removed from the machine, opened up and the cast white metal parts, still attached to the gate/sprue network, pulled clear of the tool, and the process repeated.

Assembling the *Skipjack*
After all the smoke and flurry of part

production was out of the way, I was presented with an array of GRP hull pieces, solid and hollow cast polyurethane resin pieces, and a handful of metal detail items. What to do now?

The reason the hull was done in four pieces (the hollow cast stern section, upper hull, and two lower hull pieces) was to facilitate creation of a long longitudinal break terminating at each end in half-round radial breaks. Through the two hull halves formed I would access the inside of the hull for installation, and later servicing, of the mechanisms needed to make the model a fully-capable R/C submarine. This 'Z' break between the upper and lower hull halves – the forward radial break running under the hull, the after radial break at the upper hull – permits a single machine screw aft, and a 'capture lip' forward, to hold the two hull halves together. This trick makes access to the inside to the hull a quick and simple operation.

Bonding the hull pieces
First, all GRP and resin parts were de-greased with lacquer thinner scrubbed onto the inside and outside of each part with the aid of steel wool. The upper hull/forward lower hull pieces were held together by tack gluing them with CA adhesive. Then, a small amount of catalysed epoxy resin was mixed and used to saturate a strip of fibreglass reinforcing tape which had been positioned over the inside seam between the two GRP hull pieces.

Turning to the attachment of the resin stern section to the GRP lower hull piece. Since there is more than enough lap contact area on the outer face of the cast resin tail section radial flange, gap-filling CA adhesive was found to be adequate to achieve a strong bond between those parts. Other than a few detail items, attached after painting/weathering, the bonding operations described above were the only ones needed on the *Skipjack* model!

I then opened up the bottom flood/drain holes with the aid of drill, files, and sandpaper. Remember, the model I am describing here is of the 'wet-hull' type: the interior of the hull and sail flood when

An assembled, filled, primed, and sanded *Skipjack* 'kit' ready for penetration cut-out and painting/ weathering. This is the condition I package the kit for delivery to my customers.

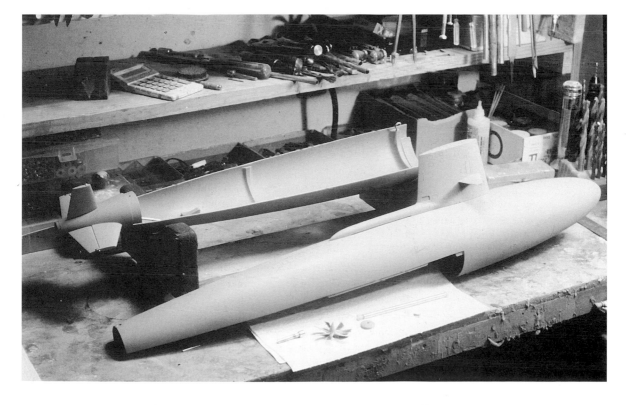

placed in the water, so no attempt is made to make the break between the hull halves or the union between the sail and hull watertight. The many flood/drain openings punched into the bottom of the *Skipjack* model are the same in shape and function as those on the original – they are vital to the model's ability to take on and discharge water as it transitions from surface to submerged trim.

The sail is secured on top of the hull with two machine screws. The sail planes (interconnected by transverse running brass shaft) press-fit into holes drilled into the sides of the sail. The two stern planes and two rudders make up to internal yokes with mechanical fasteners. The masts atop the sail are press-fits into cavities formed during the sail casting operation. The two deck capstans are likewise simple press-fits.

'Assembly' of my 1:96 *Skipjack* model parts, owing to a carefully worked-out methodology, is relatively simple and quick. It is my practice to address each separate unit as a model unto itself, thereby permitting easy accomplishment of the assembly, putty work, filing and sanding, priming, painting and weathering tasks needed to prepare the several GRP/resin/metal parts for assembly into the completed model.

Open seams (other than the breaks separating the two hull halves) were filled with Evercoat's Spot-Lite automotive putty, a two-part polyester based quick-cure paste.

The hardened filler was then smoothed with a file and descending grades of sandpaper. All units (hull, sail, fairwater planes, rudders, stern planes, antenna masts and antennas, anchor, and two capstans, and propeller) were wet-sanded with #600 sandpaper, followed by a light scrubbing with fine steel wool. All assemblies were then spray-painted with DuPont 'Lucite' brand 131S automotive lacquer primer and later wet-sanded with #600 sandpaper. Flaws identified by the gray primer were filled with Nitro-Stan touch-up putty (an air-dry lacquer-based putty, far superior to any 'hobby' putty on the market!), sanded smooth, and those areas re-shot with primer.

All sub-assemblies were then joined together until, finally, sitting on my worktable, was a completed primer-gray model of a *Skipjack*. At that stage I installed the control linkages and propulsion shaft. An outfitted and tested WTC-3 was installed. Then an amount of fixed ballast weight and buoyant foam within the lower and upper portions of the hull, respectively (the lead weight so arranged as to place the model's centre of gravity at the longitudinal centre).

The Watertight Cylinder and 'Sea Trials'

Development and use of the WTC-3
Previous R/C models of mine had featured fixed or semi-fixed watertight containers

The components of the WTC-3 and the watertight tube.

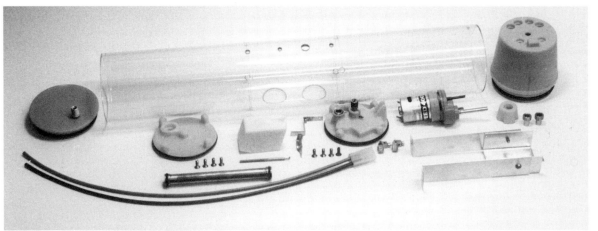

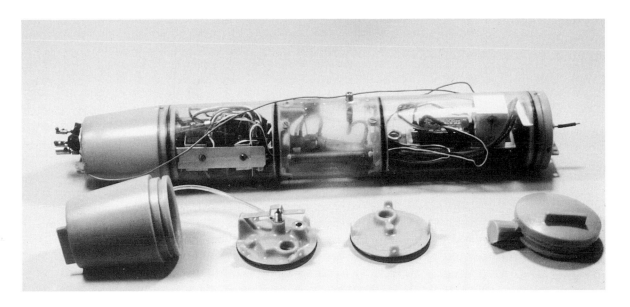

that housed the control and propulsion elements. However, as the *Skipjack* was to be our first commercially available kit – marketed in concert with a completely removable WTC system – I set about designing, building, testing and finalising the WTC-3 (3in outside diameter), a purpose-built WTC, designed to operate our 1:96 *Skipjack* and other similar-sized R/C model submarines of the wet-hull type.

The WTC-3 is basically a 19in long piece of 3in-diameter clear Lexan tube divided inside by two cast resin bulkheads. The three spaces thus formed comprise, from stern to bows, the *after dry space* which is capped at its end by the 'motor bulkhead'. This space contains the R/C system, the motor with attached three-to-one gear reduction unit, motor shaft watertight seal, stern plane and rudder servos, APC-3 angle keeper, and SubSafe 'emergency surfacing' circuit. The centre *ballast tank space* comprises the 11oz capacity gas type ballast tank, complete with actuating servo and linkages needed to operate the vent and blow valves. A conduit tube runs through the ballast tank, communicating the wiring between forward and after dry sections of the WTC. Finally, the *forward dry space* contains a standard 7.2 Volt Ni-Cad battery (the same

type used in R/C cars) and a proportional motor speed controller/BEC. The removable forward bulkhead allows for quick access to the battery for swap-out or speed controller adjustment, without necessitating the removal of the WTC from the hull. A battery change takes only 30 seconds!

The WTC fits snugly into pre-formed foundations moulded within the lower GRP hull piece and is secured there with rubber bands. An indexing backstop (another appendage cast within the lower hull) assures correct alignment of the WTC within the hull. The only interface points to the control/propulsion elements of the WTC/hull are quick connect fittings between the rudder and stern plane push-rods, and a Dumas type universal coupler for the propulsion drive train. Installation/removal of the WTC from a hull take less than a minute! Not only is the WTC-3 easily accessible for repair or adjustment, it can quickly be transferred from one submarine hull to another, making it possible, for those on a shoestring budget, to operate many different hulls from a common WTC.

It is good practice, after getting the hull to primer gray and the WTC outfitted, to integrate the two and then test out the boat in the water to work out the trim.

A completed WTC-3, the same type unit used aboard our 1:96 *Skipjack* class submarine kit.

Since the model is likely to get knocked about as sea trials proceed and changes in foam/weight are made. As it is easier to repair gray primer than a complicated paint/weathering job, it is best to let the final painting and weathering jobs wait until all the mechanical 'bugs' are worked out and the boat trimmed out to satisfaction before painting.

Radio controls

I have spent almost all of this chapter rambling on about the process of building a R/C submarine, yet I have not addressed the obvious question that pops into the mind of anyone not familiar with the practice of R/C submarining: 'How does an R/C submarine get its radio signal while submerged, and is specialised R/C equipment needed to achieve this ?'

The fact is that transmission through fresh water, to depths as great as 20ft, are possible with perfect reception by the model's receiver. However, the R/C equipment available to the hobbyist can not punch its radio signal through salt water, so operation in that medium (unless you keep a dedicated receiver antenna above the surface at all times) is all but impossible.

You can successfully operate a R/C submarine in swimming-pool water, but chemicals like chlorine will attenuate the signal, so range will be likely to be reduced to some extent – in some cases pool water will restrict your depth to as little as 3ft with a cross range of 30ft. Public pools, for obvious reasons, present you with the least radio range underwater.

I provide an external antenna on my WTCs, making up to the on-board receiver through a brass stud passing through the motor bulkhead. No attempt is made to pass the receiver antenna wire through a waterproof gland or the like. The stud ensures that no water can communicate from the external antenna to the inside of the WTC. (Even the small space between the conduction wire and its insulation on a receiver's antenna will admit pressurised water. Eventually water will reach the receiver board and short out the circuits, rendering it inoperative. I have seen this happen aboard a friend's submarine that was nearly lost when its on-board receiver flooded in just this way.)

Pictured below you see two antenna schemes I favour. One just lets you string out the antenna the length of the hull (GRP

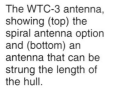

The WTC-3 antenna, showing (top) the spiral antenna option and (bottom) an antenna that can be strung the length of the hull.

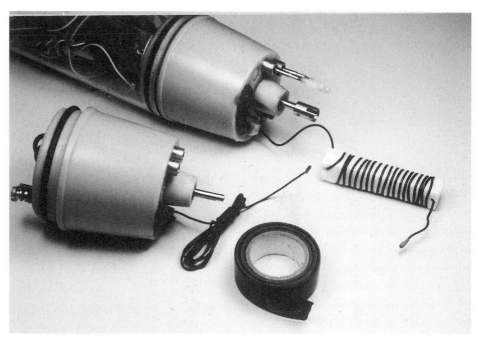

is basically transparent to radio frequencies, so there is no need to route the antenna externally of the hull). A more convenient means of rigging the antenna is to wrap it around a non-conductor, such as a foam core, in a spiral fashion. As long as none of the antenna wire crosses itself this scheme seems to offer no appreciable loss of receiver sensitivity or selectivity to the transmitter – range with the spiral-wound antenna is nearly as good as with the antenna wire strung out. So, in fact, the question is not how far the radio signal will travel in water, but how deep/far away can the operator see his model. Submarines travelling underwater can sometimes be pretty hard to see! Visibility (or the lack of it) is what limits the range from which the model submarine can be controlled.

As to the radio control transmitter and receiver themselves, standard, unmodified commercial gear is used. Of course the radio must operate at a specific frequency within a government-approved 'surface vehicle only' radio band. R/C gear for model submarines is purchased at the same sources used to acquire your other hobby-related items.

Static stability

Static stability, the submarine's ability to right itself when upset in the roll or pitch plane, is dependent on the vertical alignment and distance apart of two opposing forces. One force line, referred to as the centre of gravity, represents the accumulated gravitic force and exerts downwards. The other, the centre of buoyancy, represents the accumulated upward, buoyant forces. Static stability

The *Skipjack* under water. This is a completed model - sea trials should be undertaken before the final paintwork is finished.

exists when these two force lines are vertically aligned, with the centre of buoyancy (c.b.) above the centre of gravity (c.g.). The greater the vertical distance between the c.g. and c.b, the greater the roll and pitch righting moments, and the more statically stable the submarine is.

A considerable amount of weight, in the form of cast lead, is placed low in the model submarine's hull, and countering that weight is buoyant foam placed high in the hull – low c.g./high c.b. In practice the weight is installed first, then moved longitudinally until the longitudinal c.g. is about centre of the hull. The amount of weight and its longitudinal position is determined through experiment as the model is trimmed out in the water.

As a submarine has no control surface to effect righting forces about the roll axis, it counts entirely on its static stability about that axis to right itself when a torque force – propeller torque or sail 'foil roll', for example – upsets the submarine about the roll axis. However, it must be pointed out here that static stability forces are no match against stern plane or hull-induced pitching forces at any but the lowest underwater speeds.

Setting surface and submerged trim

Determining the amount and placement of the buoyant foam is conveniently done by holding foam pieces against the outside of the hull with rubber bands. Later, once determination is complete, the foam blocks are placed within the hull and secured with RTV adhesive (bathtub caulk). Remember that no foam is placed higher than the model's designed waterline. The model is then returned to the water and the ballast tank is flooded.

Good submerged trim is achieved on a small R/C submarine model such as this *Skipjack* when about ½in of sail projects into the air, with the model resting on an 'even keel'. Surface trim of the model, with the ballast tank empty, puts the waterline at the designed waterline of the *Skipjack* class. It was determined through experiment

(during the 'trials' phase of *WTC-3* development) that only 11oz of water ballast was needed to achieve this level of buoyancy.

Sea trials

Model submarines representing modern round-hulls, like their big brothers, do not handle well on the surface. Remember, nearly half of the model's rudder area is out of the water in surface trim, and, at speed on the surface, much more thrust is needed to counter the 'wave-forming' drag than to maintain an equivalent speed underwater. Submerged the submarine will give up this parasitic wave-making drag at a depth deeper than three times its diameter. However, running shallow at periscope depth is deep enough to realise a huge drop in total drag. This is observed by doing the following: leaving the throttle alone, command a dive by venting the ballast tank and manipulating the stern planes. As the model dips below the surface you will notice a marked increase in speed as the vehicle sheds itself of the wave-making parasitic drag.

After running the model around on the surface for a while, the ballast tank is vented and as the model sinks, the stern planes are worked to keep the sunken model at periscope depth – just the tip of the periscope projecting out of the water. The throttle is played with as the ways of the model are learned – with a speedy boat like this little *Skipjack* too much power applied to the propeller will quickly send it out of control.

Underwater is where this submarine belongs. Beneath the waves the *Skipjack* turns tighter, runs faster, and is much easier to control – providing that the rudder is not pushed over too much above a critical speed. To do so is to risk complete loss of control. My little *Skipjack* is fast and turns on a dime – but it is a vessel that requires the operator's complete and undivided attention! The boat is surfaced by blowing the ballast tank dry and then it is driven around some more, submerged, surfaced,

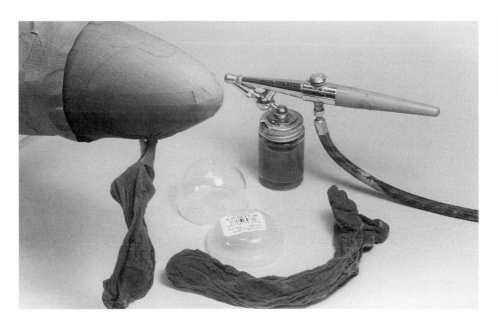

Use of a stretched nylon stocking to form the geodetic pattern atop the light coloured sonar domes.

and 'played with' as its performance characteristics are revealed and appreciated.

After the trimming and initial in-water tests, the model was then brought back to the shop where the WTC was removed and serviced, the sail and other appendages removed, and the exterior of all parts scrubbed with soap and water, rinsed, and dried. At that point any damaged areas were attended to with filler, putty, files and sandpaper and primer. At that point the gray model was ready for its paint job, weathering, markings, and finally, display.

Painting, Detailing and Weathering the Model

The real *Skipjack* submarines, fresh off the building blocks, featured a scheme of anti-fouling red paint from the waterline down and black from centreline up. The two deck-mounted escape trunk buoy fairings were painted 'international orange' and the white hull numbers prominently painted on each side of the sail (and in some cases, smaller hull numbers near the bow as well).

However, after sea-trials and following the boat's acceptance by the Navy, the red/black demarcation line was shifted to the centreline, the buoy fairings painted black, and the hull numbers on the sail painted out. In fact the only distinctive 'colours' on an operational *Skipjack* were the draft numbers painted on the hull and upper rudder. All these measures were taken on operational boats to make them less observable from the air (and space-based) ASW platforms.

Obviously a model submarine is not at any risk from air attack (seagulls don't count!), and should be painted with maximum visibility as a primary objective, though I tend to make subtle (and sometimes not so subtle) concessions to reality when painting and weathering a R/C scale model submarine such as this. So, in keeping with that objective, I favour the pre-commissioning scheme. It presents more anti-fouling red and I also retain the hull numbers and brightly-coloured escape buoys. When the submerged model is below periscope depth and out some distance away from shore, you need all the visual clues to the model's location you can get!

The Basic Red/Black Paint Application
I favour the Krylon brand spray-cans. Their 'sandible red primer' is a dead ringer for the brownish-red anti-fouling colour. I apply it straight from the can to the areas on the hull, stern planes, anchor rudder at and

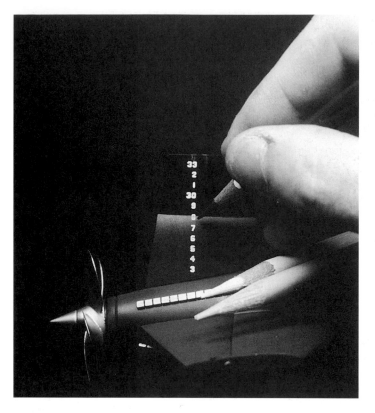

Use of coloured pencils to represent the green and off-white discoloration seen near the submarines waterline. The pencil work began only after the upper surfaces of the hull and upper rudder had been masked and off-white sprayed down from the tape's edge, and the masking removed. Freehand use of the spray-brush a few scale feet below the waterline, this time loaded with a green shade of anti-foul red, represented the 'banding' so often observed below the waterline.

Additionally, the dark gray causes the 'weathering' applied later to stand in sharp contrast to it.

With the model painted in red/black and a custom-made dry-transfer marking set used to achieve the draft numbers and hull numbers, the model assemblies are given a clear coat, the sub-assembles re-assembled and the job would seem to be done. But not for me!

Creative masking and painting

As I researched the *Skipjack* design, some photos showed light-coloured sonar windows at the bow, while others did not. I elected, in keeping with the desire to make my model more visible as it travelled underwater, to paint these structures a light shade of gray. While masking and painting the sonar windows I took it one step further and represented a 'grid' pattern onto them, suggesting a slight dishing of the windows down onto the geodesic metal strengthening foundation beneath the real things.

After masking to the engraved outlines of the two sonar windows (one above the torpedo tubes, the other below), a nylon stocking was stretched over the windows and light gray spray-painted through the stocking weave onto the window's surface. With the stocking and tape masking removed a neat looking geodesic pattern upon the two gray sonar windows was revealed. A neat trick!

Much 'character' can be added to effect a 'in use' look to a model through the practised and careful application of ground chalks, artist's coloured pencils, oil paints (applied and worked with stippling brushes), abrasives, spray-brush, texture sponges and sticks. A well-executed weathering job can make a model, but a poorly-done one can ruin it. Note the subtle streaking of off-black running from the periscope/mast wells down the sides of the sail, as well as some running rust from the fairwater plane operating shaft and slight signs of wear around the scribed-in access plates and doors.

below the surface trim waterline – not worrying about overspray. The Krylon paint dries quickly and is tough enough not to pull up with the masking tape applied later. The hull was then mounted on a level workbench and, using a surface gauge loaded with a soft lead pencil, the waterline marked onto its surface - not forgetting to temporarily mount the upper rudder to the hull so its red/black demarcation line is marked off as well.

Using low-tack masking tape the lower portion of the hull and rudder were masked off, the upper edge of the masking tape falling along the pencilled waterlines. Time to lay down the black. This is where I exhibit a little 'artistic license'. Instead of simply painting the above-waterline portions of the model a true black, I used a very, very dark gray instead, allowing for scale-effect – the apparent lightening of a surface as the observer distances himself from the subject. Painting the model black simply turns the model into a silhouette, almost impossible to see underwater.

Aboard the real boats, on the above-waterline structure, running water flows down, following the path of least resistance, soon 'streaking' all topside surfaces with residue, vertical streaking on flat surfaces (like the sail and rudder) and radial bands on rounded surfaces (the hull). My favourite streaking medium is linseed-based, turpentine-cut oil paints. Black oil paint and black doped with just a touch of white work well together when adjacent patches are streaked onto the model and blended slightly against each other. The slow-dry oil paints, when used sparingly, achieve the most subtle and striking weathering effects. Once the waterline had been spray-painted onto the hull and upper rudder I used green and off-white artist's pencils to represent the discoloration seen at and slightly below the submarines surface trim waterline.

Study of photos of dry-docked submarines reveal a form of hull weathering unique to bodies that experience long-term

exposure to water, namely discoloration of the below-waterline portions of the hull in the form of a series of horizontal bands, running the entire length of the hull and upper rudder. For example, just at the waterline is a very light, almost white, narrow band of bleached out 'sea grass'. Just below that is a band of green sea grass. Farther down the hull is observed a wider band of a patchy brownish-green marine growth.

To achieve these patchy horizontal bands of discoloration on the hull I first take some liquid soap, dip a stipple brush into it, wipe off most of the excess soap from the fibres, then stipple random areas of the below waterline hull and upper rudder. The soap is left to dry. I then shoot the hull with horizontal bands of well-thinned anti-foul red/light gray, anti-foul red/green-brown, then finally anti-foul red/gray. After these bands had dried I wiped the surfaces with a damp paper towel, dissolving soap masking revealing

Brass propellers don't remain a shiny brass color in salt water very long! Quickly they dull out and gather a 'speckling' of oxidized metal. I represented this by loading a stiff toothbrush with a lightened shade of brass paint, aimed the brush at the brass colored propeller, and let fly by stroking the bristles with my thumb. A quick, messy way to achieve the speckling needed! (See the colour section for the result.)

the rough, distortions of the horizontal bands seen in the reference photos. Soap is just one form of liquid masking agent. I have also employed toothpaste, Vaseline, PVA, and other mediums in this capacity as well.

Brass propellers and other copper-bearing alloys do not remain a shiny 'gold' colour very long when subjected to immersion in salt water. Such metals evidence light coloured patches across their surface. Brass propellers, such as those employed on the *Skipjack*s, also quickly gain an oxidised coat. I represented this oxidation on my gold-painted propeller by loading a stiff toothbrush with a lightened shade of the gold, aiming the brush at the propeller, and let fly little blobs of the paint by stroking the brush bristles with my thumb. A quick, if messy, way to achieve the speckling needed!

Near the top of the sail, at the leading edge, are four deadlights (windows). Masking was applied around them and they were painted a light shade of gray. Two escape buoys on deck had to be painted

'international orange'. The areas of hull around those two items were masked off and the buoys painted.

A submarine's deck can get pretty slick. So, to afford better traction for deck hands, those areas on the submarine's surface subject to foot traffic were given an undercoat of a very gritty coating referred to as 'non-skid'. The non-skid was laid down then over-coated with the basic black hull paint. On my model I represent the non-skid areas by masking around the deck and sail planes and laying down a coat of slightly lightened black. This represented the slightly different reflective quality of the rough non-skid standing in contrast to the adjacent smooth surfaces covered with the same paint.

The painting and weathering complete, I applied custom made dry-transfer markings I had made by Archer Fine Transfers to the upper rudder, sail, and hull. A heavy clear coat doped with a flattening agent completed the painting/weathering process and the model was ready for display.

Sources

Chapter 1: Large-Scale Working Models: HMS *Warrior* 1860, by William Mowll

Mowell, William, *Building a Working Model Warship: HMS Warrior 1860* (London 1997)

Old Maritime Books
Rare and out of print.
Frank Smith, 100 Heaton Rd, Newcastle NE6 5HL.
Tel: 0191 265 6333.
John Lewcock, 6 Chewell's Lane, Haddenham, Ely, Cambs CB6 3SS
Tel: 01353 741960.
E-mail: lewcok@ maritime-bookseller.com

New Nautical Books
Chatham Publishing: for catalogue contact -
The Marketing Department, Chatham Publishing, 61 Frith Street, London W1D 3JL
Tel: 020 7434 4242
Fax: 020 7434 4415
Website: www.chathampublishing.com

Model Boats magazine (monthly), published by Nexus Specialist Interests, Azalea Drive, Swanley, Kent BR8 8HU
Tel: 01322 660070
Website: www.modelboats.co.uk
  - for all sorts of relevant information and advertising, suppliers etc. Their Plans department has modelmakers' plans of both HMS *Warrior* and the *Discovery*.

Chapter 2: Waterline Laminated Balsa Models: HMS *Ocean* 1900, by Eric Dyke

Commissioning Book of HMS Ocean, by kind permission of the Commanding Officer.
Burt, R A, *British Battleships 1889-1904* (London 1989)
Chant, Christopher, *History of the World's Warships* (Anglesey 2001)
Ellis, Richard, *The Royal Navy at Malta*, Volume 1 (Liskeard 1989)
Gibbons, Tony, *The Complete Encyclopaedia of Battleships and Battlecruisers* (London 1983)

Chapter 3: Modelling an Inter-War Aircraft Carrier: HMS *Glorious* 1936, by Brian King

Original Plans of HMS Glorious
The following plans were obtained from the National Maritime Museum, Greenwich, London. All 'as fitted'.

MCD 20350/1 profile starboard side
MCD 20350/2 upper gallery, flight and bridge decks
MCD 20350/3 upper hangar and lower gallery decks
MCD 20350/4 lower hangar and upper decks
MCD 20350/5 main and lower decks
MCD 20350/6 platform deck and holds
MCD 20350/7 sections
MCD 20374 docking plan
MCD 20382 rigging sketch

Published Sources
Campbell, John, *Naval Weapons of WW2* (London 1985)
King, Brian, *Advanced Ship Modelling* (London 2000)
------------, and Watkin, Azien, *Photo Etching* (Nexus workshop series: New York 2002)
Model Shipwright Nos. 103, 104.
Society of Friends of the Fleet Air Arm Museum, *80 Years of the British Aircraft Carrier (1914 to 1994)* (London 1994)
Thetford, Owen, *British Naval Aircraft since 1912* (London 1958)
Winton, John, *Carrier Glorious* (London 1958)

Chapter 4: Scratch-Building Second World War Capital Ships in Plastic Card: HMS *Hood* 1941, by Peter Beisheim

Published Sources
Burt, R A, *British Battleships 1919-1939* (London 1993)
Jurens, W J, 'The Loss of HMS *Hood* - a Re-examination', *Warship International 2* (1987)
Monografie Morskie No 6: *Hood* (Gdyma 1999)
Raven Alan, *Warship Perspectives: Camouflage* Vol. 1-2, Royal Navy 1939 – 1941 and 1942 (WR Press 2001)

----------, and Roberts, John, *British Battleships of World War II* (London 1976)

Roberts, John, *Anatomy of the Ship: The Battlecruiser Hood* (London 1982)

Sowinski, Larry, *US Navy Camouflage of the World War Two Era* (Floating Dry Dock 1976)

Warship Profile No. 19 HMS Hood Battle Cruiser 1916–1941 (Windsor 1972)

Wlliams, David, *Naval Camouflage 1914-1945: A Complete Visual Reference* (London 2001)

Winklareth, Robert J, *The Bismarck Chase* (London 1999)

Websites

HMS *Hood* Association
website: www.hmshood.com

Chapter 5: Miniature Warships of the Second World War, by Philip Baggaley

These sources comprise plans, which may or may not be produced for modellers' books, periodicals and photographs. It is only practical to list certain suppliers and I have found that acquiring information about a warship always proceeds at an erratic pace and there is often and element of luck or chance involved.

Plans

British Warships

(i) David Macgregor Plans, 12 Upper Oldfield Park, Bath, Avon, BA2 3JZ

David Macgregor supplies Norman Ough's excellent plans of about twenty inter-war and wartime British warships from battleships to submarines. He also supplies plans by John Lambert and others covering smaller vessels such as minesweepers, trawlers and MTBs.

(ii) The Maritime Information Centre, The National Maritime Museum, Park Row, Greenwich, London, SE10 9NF

The National Maritime Museum has a very extensive collection of Second World War British warship plans, but as these are usually large scale ones, these can be expensive for making a miniature model.

(iii) Sambrook Maritime Models, 214 Ruxley Lane, West Ewell, Surrey, KT19 9EZ

Sambrook Maritime supplies A & A plans of Second World War British warships.

French Warships

L'Association des Amis des Museé de la Marine, Palais de Chaillot, 75116 Paris, France

The Association supplies a limited range of plans of Second World War French warships. The only plan that I have used, the 1:100 plan of the battleship *Richelieu*, was excellent.

American Warships

The Floating Drydock, c/o General Delivery, Kresgeville, Pennsylvania 18333, USA

They stock a huge range of plans of American Second World War warships to numerous scales and they also supply photographs and camouflage designs.

German Warships

David Macgregor Plans, Sambrook Maritime and the Floating Drydock all supply plans of Second World War German warships.

Japanese Warships

Pacific Front Hobbies, PO Box 2098, Roseburg, Oregon 97470, USA

They stock a large range of plans of Japanese Second World War Warships. In the last few years three ranges of Polish warship monographs have been published covering various Second World War Japanese warships. The monograph series are known as *Okrety Swiata*, *Monographie Morskie* and *Profile Morskie*. The latter contain a centre spread plan, colour drawings on the cover and pages of superstructure plans and drawings of detailed parts.

Subject to limited imports of stock these monographs can be obtained from: -

(i) Midland Counties Publications, Unit 3 Maizefield, Hinckley, Leics, LE10 1YF

(ii) Barbarossa Books, 242 High Street, Bromley, Kent, BR1 1PQ

(iii) Books International, 101 Lynchford Road, Farnborough, Hants, GU14 6ET

For plans and information about lesser-known foreign warships, it is well worth correspondence with a modeller overseas, if one can be found. Usually the correspondence starts with a letter from an overseas modeller in a modelling magazine requesting information. If you can assist you reply and then keep in touch. In this way I have made contact with a Polish modeller and much of the information for my Japanese models comes from him.

Books

I will only refer to monographs on particular warships, which would be useful to modellers rather than the more general naval reference books. Conway Maritime Press produce the hardback 'Anatomy of the Ship' series with extremely detailed drawings of every part of a particular warship. The series have covered British, American, German, Italian and Japanese vessels, but only the more recent books remain in print.

Turning to soft-back publications, some of the Polish monographs referred to above cover British warships. British warships were also covered in the *Warship Profiles, Ensign* and *Man O' War* series,which are all out of print, but which can sometimes be obtained from secondhand maritime bookshops.

There are various current series of landscape style American publications covering American warships. These are Floating Drydock's *Warship Data*, Leeward *Publications* Ship's *Data, Warships Pictorial*, and Squadron/Signal Publications Warships series. The latter covers classes of ships, eg battleships or *Essex* class carriers, rather than individual vessels.

German warships arc covered by the German *Marine Arsenal* series and a few by Conway's *Maritime Modellers* series. Italian warships are covered by the Orizzonte Mare series, some of which cover the technical side of a vessel and others its operational history. The Polish monographs, referred to under plans above, include Japanese warships.

Photographs

British Warships

National Maritime Museum – For address see under Plans above.

Imperial War Museum, Lambeth Road, London, SE1 6HZ

The IWM has an extensive collection of photographs of British warships in WWII

French Warships

Editions Marius Bar – 491 Avenue Marceau, 83100 Toulon, France

I do not know the range of photographs stocked here, but their photographs of the *Richelieu* were of superb quality.

American Warships

The Floating Drydock (for address see under Plans above) have an extensive range of photographs of American warships.

Other Nationalities

I have only used photographs from books, magazines and periodicals.

Chapter 6: Model Warships from Plastic Kits, by Loren Perry

Ashey, Mike, *Basics of Ship Modelling – The Illustrated Guide* (Waukesha, WI 2000)

----------, *Building and Detailing Scale Model Ships* (Waukesha, WI 1996)

Friedman, Norman, *Naval Radar* (London 1981)

----------, *World's Naval Weapons Systems* (Annapolis 1989)

Perry, Loren, *Photoetching for the Plastic Ship Modeller* (Lopez, WA 1987)

Polmar, Norman, *Ships and Aircraft of the US Fleet* (various editions, Annapolis 1965-1997)

Chapter 7: Working Model Small Craft: Sub-chaser *SC 1055*, by David Jack

Doscher, J Henry Jnr, *Subchaser in the South Pacific* (Eakin Press 1994)

Lambert, John and Ross, Al, *Allied Coastal Forces Volume 1* (London 1994)

Roberts, Douglas and Scheina, R L, *The Splendid Five* (Annapolis 1980)

Treadwell, Theodore R, *Splinter Fleet* (Annapolis 2000)

US Coast Guard Cutters and Craft of WW2 (Annapolis 1982)

Chapter 8: Large-Scale Static Display Models: USS *Enterprise* 1975, by Stephen W Henninger

Gillmer, Thomas C, *Modern Ship Design* (Annapolis 1970)

US Navy, *USS Enterprise Cruise Book* 1972-73

----------, *USS Enterprise Cruise Book* 1974-75

Wingate, John, *Warships in Profile* (Windsor 1973)

Chapter 9: Radio-Controlled Model Submarines: USS *Skipjack* 1959, by David Merriman, III

Plans, Video Tapes, Associations, Referrence Material

The Subcommittee (association, quarterly magazine) SubCommittee Membership, P.O. Box 28372, Parkville, MD 21234-8373 USA

Website:

www.subcommittee.com

   SeaPhoto (photo reference), 1145 Oakwood Drive, Millbrae, CA 94030 USA

Tel: 650-225-9466

Website:

www:http://members.aol.com/seaphoto/index.html

   Deep Sea Design (plans), 841 Leslie Drive, Victoria, British Columbia,

V8X 2Y3, Canada.

Tel: 250-475-0348

   The Floating Drydock (plans, photos, books), c/o General Delivery,

Kresgeville, PA 18333.

Tel: 610-381-2004

Website:

www.floatingdrydock.com

   Taubman Plane Service (plans), 11 College Drive, #4G, Jersey City, NJ, USA

Website:

www.modelersboatyard.com/taubmans/taubman1.htm

   Ray Mason Productions (video), 9 Pine Drive East, Nesconset, NY, USA

Tel: 516-585-5715

D&E Miniatures (video), 835 Holly Hedge Ave., Virginia

Beach, VA 23452.

Tel: 757-468-4687

Website:

www.vabiz.com/d&e

   Traplet Publications (*Simply Submarines and Model SubmarineTechnology*), 3105 Tatman Court, Suite 105, Urbana, IL, USA

Tel: 217-328-4444

Website:

www.traplet.com

Index

Page references in *italics* refer to illustrations

Abbreviations:

Fr = France; GB = British merchant ship; Ger = Germany; HMS = His/Her Majesty's Ship; It = Italy;
Jpn = Japan; USS = United States Ship